Everybody's Guide
to
Plate Collecting

Everybody's Guide
to
Plate Collecting

Second Edition

Herschell Lewis and Margo Lewis

Bonus Books, Inc., Chicago

98   97   96   95   94   5   4   3   2   1

Library of Congress Catalog Card Number: 94-70119

International Standard Book Number: 1-56625-007-2

Bonus Books, Inc.
160 East Illinois Street, Chicago, Illinois 60611

Printed in the United States of America

Contents

Contents _____

Preface

Who would expect major upheavals and changes over a short five-year span, in a field as placid and stable as plate collecting!

But that's exactly what happened between the years 1989 and 1994.

First of all, the Norman Rockwell boom has lost much of its steam. The name Rockwell on a plate isn't, in the year 1994, an automatic guarantee of wild plate-buying. (What is? The name Elvis Presley, an indication of the temporal impact of trends.)

Why? Chapter 18—new for this edition—dissects this trend-in-reverse.

Second, we have a whole new generation of plate collectors who weren't even in our ranks when the first edition of *Everybody's Guide to Plate Collecting* was published. Their interests aren't always parallel to those of the old-timers.

Third, plate collecting has been tried in the crucible...has been singed on both sides...and has emerged with a new strength. In the period from 1989 to 1992, few producers were issuing plates. The most collected art form went into near-eclipse. Many of the best-established artists had to go fishing around for a new home; some of these never did find a home, resulting in a quiet disappearance from the plate collecting scene.

Retailers took the biggest hit during this recent "plate recession." Their customers reversed the flow.

Instead of buying plates, collectors arrived at dealers' doorsteps with plates in hand, looking to sell those plates at published prices which no dealer could pay. Hard times!

So the dealer market in the mid-to-late 1990s has dwindled to minor-league status. The new collectors respond to *direct* advertising in publications and broadcast media.

As these new collectors settle into place, the dealer market may, to some extent, rebuild itself. But because the major force now belongs to companies who sell their plates direct, dealers no longer control lines of distribution.

What's hot and what's not? What will come of it all in the twenty-first century? Check your opinion against ours—again, in chapter 18.

—Herschell and Margo Lewis
Plantation, Florida, 1994

Acknowledgments

Our thanks to Ms. Pat Owen for making available photographs and for sharing her vast knowledge of plate collecting. Pat, with her husband Murnie ("Buzz") Owen, owns and operates Viking Import House, one of the pioneer collectibles sources in the United States.

To Lorraine Stone, also of Viking Imports, our deep appreciation for the many hours spent tracking down exhibits.

Preparation of this text would have taken months longer had we not had the help of Peggy Nelson in organizing facts, examples, and quotations.

Most of all, our thanks to the plate producers with whom we've had the honor of working over the years—The Bradford Exchange, Calhoun's Collectors Society, The Hamilton Collection, Heritage House, the United States Historical Society, Bing & Grøndahl-Royal Copenhagen, and the no-longer-existent but much-missed Ghent Collection.

Note: Some of the information in this book appeared in a different form in our regular columns in the magazine *Plate World*. We appreciate that publication's cooperation.

Margo and Herschell Lewis
Plantation, Florida

Chapter 1

What's White and Smooth and Goes "Ping!"?
(The Natural History of Porcelain)

We plate collectors have a lot in common with Marco Polo, Frederick the Great, Madame Pompadour, Napoleon, J.P. Morgan, and Samuel Clemens. Our love of the smooth white surface with pretty pictures on it also makes us confrères of kings, emperors, sultans, mandarins, and presidents.

Since the seventh century, porcelain not only has held a fascination for those who love exquisite works of art; it has spurred the urge to own it.

Just what exactly is porcelain? Why has its beauty and permanence held a magic allure since it first was created in China more than 1300 years ago?

The Origin of Porcelain

The remarkable T'ang Dynasty, which ruled China for nearly 300 years (618-907 A.D.), introduced porcelain to an astonished world. Magic? That's exactly what travelers thought. When they could, they smuggled precious pieces of porcelain out of China into Europe, where it became a symbol of affluence, much admired and frequently the most valuable art treasure.

Until the T'ang Dynasty the only ceramic anyone could make was the "low-fired" clay-bodied cooking vessels and decorative pots. The world had seen those since caveman days.

The Chinese always had been innovators. An art gallery in Washington, D.C. has an example of white stoneware fired around 1400 B.C.! And glazing began about 400 years before the first porcelain pieces were fired.

What was different about the first true porcelain fired in "china stone"?

First, it was the stone itself—actually petuntse, a kind of feldspar. ("Petuntse" is the French way of pronouncing "pai-tun-tzu," which in Chinese is self-explanatory: *pai* means "white," *tun* means "mound," and *tzu* means "derived from" or "offspring of." See the connection?) Somehow a wise Chinese got the idea of mixing it with a strange white clay found in the Kao-ling district. You can see where the word kaolin, meaning clay, came from—compressing Kaoling together. Kaolin is actually decomposed feldspathic rock, with a high concentration of aluminum silicate. That isn't what made it special to early potters, who were sick and tired of the porosity and fragility of their clay pots. What made kaolin the clay of history was the wonderful change in it when it was fired at high temperatures—temperatures that would shatter regular clay pots. It hardened into a tight, dense, tough, impermeable substance keeping the shape of whatever mold it might have been in when it was heated. And it was translucent.

Marco Polo's Contribution

Among the many legacies civilization can trace to Marco Polo is the word porcelain itself. He called the translucent ceramic *porcellana*, the Italian word for the smooth, pearly cowrie shell.

Marco Polo visited China during the reign of Kublai Khan, the farsighted Mongol who founded the Yuan Dynasty. This was a short-lived dynasty—1280 to 1368—but its effect on human history was enormous.

The T'ang Dynasty had been followed by the Sung Dynasty (960-1279 A.D.), during which porcelain-making came to full flower. It was during the Sung Dynasty that celadon appeared—a green/gray color which a few of today's famous porcelain houses, such as Haviland, have been able to replicate. But the brief Yuan Dynasty gave the world underglaze, using the cobalt blue that has become the most familiar of all porcelain colorations.

Marco Polo brought his porcelains back to Venice and to the western nations, setting off a mad search for the Kao-ling clays. Ultimately, pockets of the clay were unearthed in France, Germany, Britain, Czechoslovakia, Japan, and the United States—all of whom became leaders in porcelain production.

The Exquisite Ming Porcelains

In 1368 the Mongol head of the Yuan Dynasty was unseated and replaced by a new emperor who founded the renowned Ming Dynasty. From 1368 until 1644, when Ch'ing succeeded Ming, China turned out its most glorious porcelains, many of which still grace museums, colors unfaded and glazes intact and uncracked.

An entire factory dedicated itself to keeping Ming emperors supplied with porcelains—so much so that stoneware almost disappeared in the imperial households.

During the Ming Dynasty constant experimentation resulted in substances other than cobalt which would impart permanent coloration during firing.

Hand painting became an acknowledged art, with reds, browns, yellows, and gold adding chromatic radiance to the ever-present cobalt blue.

Dimensional pieces were the most sought-after during this period, but plates were the most useful porcelains, being not only decorative but functional. Porcelain containers, too, were as functional as they were decorative. Expensive oils and fragrances were kept in highly-decorated vases, jars, and bowls. Sculptured pieces such as horses and warriors served a religious purpose, often being buried with emperors and nobles as protectors in the afterlife.

China began exporting porcelains in great numbers. Contrary to folklore which has given an enchanted aura to the word "Ming," many of these pieces were inferior, out-of-round, off-center, off-balance, and poorly painted. So there's Ming—and there's *Ming*.

After Ming, We Have Ch'ing

The last period of Chinese dominance in porcelain-making was the Ch'ing Dynasty, which immediately followed Ming. Ch'ing, in fact, dates from 1644 all the way up to 1911, and it brought the industry to full flower.

Ch'ing pieces are common today. Sure, they're valuable, but if you come across one in a dusty store don't let an antiques-sharpie charge you more than it's worth. Some of these pieces were made in the 20th century; even though the word "Dynasty" does apply, these porcelains don't have a Marco Polo provenance.

One notable contribution of the Ch'ing Dynasty is the "shoulder" on a plate (most collector's plates are coupe-shape, with no shoulder). This was originally designed to hold condiments. A few had been fired during the Ming Dynasty, but Ch'ing potters made the shoulder plate standard.

To many purists, the Golden Era of the Ch'ing Dynasty was the period 1650-1750. Earlier porcelains, they claim, mirrored the schlockiness and careless detail one sees in the worst of Ming; later porcelains, although slicker and more technically perfect, lack artistic originality and flair.

Europe Produces Its Own

By the mid-18th century Europe was producing tons of porcelain, but purists still demanded china from China.

It might seem odd that the emperor Augustus the Strong (Augustus II of Saxony and Poland), born in Dresden, bypassed the exquisite pieces being created in his own backyard. But porcelain from China was far more fashionable than porcelain from Dresden or Meissen.

Contrarily, Meissen china found a ready market in, of all places, China. Chinese porcelain-makers began to imitate the Meissen designs, and this may have been the beginning of the end for Chinese dominance in porcelain.

Still, during this period the industry was far advanced in China. Deep-colored translucent enamels, crackle finishes, and hand painting so elaborate it rivalled fine art on canvas—these set a standard any imitator found technically and artistically impossible to match...

...Until the great late-18th century surge, led by the cities of Meissen and Sèvres, which made Chinese china unfashionable.

The first porcelain firings in the western world were at the Meissen pottery in Germany, in the year 1707. Meissen had experimented with kaolin formulations for more than 30 years before finding a mixture which rivalled the Chinese.

At the Leipzig Fair in 1713, Meissen porcelains created a sensation and generated orders which firmly established Meissen as a porcelain fountainhead.

Venetian potters had sold soft-paste porcelains since 1575; when Meissen hard-paste porcelains appeared, Venice quickly followed, and by 1720 Venetian porcelains were making their place in the world market.

French Porcelains

In 1738 France had begun production of soft-paste porcelain at Vincennes; 18 years later the entire operation moved to Sèvres.

The city of Sèvres had two advantages as a porcelain source (initially of soft-paste and later of hard-paste): First, Sèvres had a "pool" of ceramic artists, who created pieces of wondrous elegance and beauty with spectacular "ground" (background) colors. Second, King Louis XV was one of the owners of the factory, which added a psychological value to its competitive position in the marketplace.

In 1769 huge deposits of kaolin were found near the city of Limoges. Quickly, hard-paste obsolesced soft-paste, and by 1804 no major French producer still turned out soft-paste pieces (although Sèvres returned to soft-paste and reintroduced its famous biscuit figurines half a century later).

British Porcelains

In 1671 a potter named John Dwight was awarded a patent for making porcelain and stoneware. His stoneware imitated the heavy salt-glazed Germanware which had been popular for centuries. Despite the patents, as far as anyone knows he never did make any true porcelains.

"Agateware"—a composite of various clays—appeared in Staffordshire after 1725. A few years later Ralph Wood introduced "creamware," a form of lead-glazed earthenware.

The most famous 18th century British potter was Josiah Wedgwood. Born in 1730, he began producing artistic pieces about 1754.

"Jasperware," Wedgwood's most popular product, isn't porcelain, as you know if you've handled it. Rather, it's a porous form of unglazed stoneware. Wedgwood also produced a popular line of creamware, and when Queen Charlotte (wife of King George III, the controversial monarch who prompted the American revolution) became his customer, Wedgwood's fortunes soared.

True British porcelains date from the mid-1750s, at Derby and Chelsea. Most historians credit Josiah Spode with inventing "bone china" in 1800, but the technique of adding calcined bones to porcelain dates from 1750. The difference was that Spode's formulation was for *hard*-paste porcelain.

The Rise of the Great Porcelain Houses

In England, the village Stoke-Upon-Trent, where both Wedgwood and Spode had built factories, became the center of porcelain production. Minton began operation in 1793 at Stoke.

Worcester also became a production center, becoming the home in 1786 of—what else?—Royal Worcester. Doulton was a London company, founded much later (about 1860).

In France, the American china-importer David Haviland built a factory in Limoges in 1842.

By the mid-19th century the porcelain industry had spread throughout Europe. Bing & Grøndahl was founded in 1853 and Royal Copenhagen, dating from 1775 and controlled by the crown since 1779, became a private company in 1867. Hungary (Herend), Austria, Norway (Rorstrand), Czechoslovakia, Russia (which at the height of the Czars had 70 factories), Switzerland, Ireland (Belleek), and Belgium had thriving porcelain industries. The venerable Ginori factory, near Florence (now known as Richard-Ginori), added hard-paste porcelain to its line.

In Germany, The Bayreuth and Selb areas of Bavaria became home to some of the best-known names in porcelain, such as Rosenthal and Royal Bayreuth. Hutschenreuther had opened up the area in 1814 after kaolin deposits first were found there.

Kaiser began firing porcelain in 1872, in the Bavarian town of Coburg. Villeroy & Boch built its factory near Saarbrucken, closer to the French border.

Japan, which discovered kaolin deposits at Arita, built a mammoth porcelain industry there and at Nagoya. Since World War II, Japan has emerged as a principal source of fine porcelains. Its factories are modern and capable of tremendous production capacity.

Brazil also has become a porcelain-producing country, but volume is not of great consequence in today's marketplace.

In the United States...

The early American potters settled in the region around the Pennsylvania-Ohio border—at Newcastle, Pennsylvania, and East Liverpool, Ohio.

Although porcelain-making came late to the United States, history admits that a man named Andre Duché was the first U.S. porcelain-maker, in 1741. As an industry, porcelain-making dates from 1826, when William Tucker started a factory in Philadelphia.

Actually, most American whiteware has been china, not porcelain. The difference—well, that's another story, in another chapter.

Norton & Fenton began making "parian ware"—an unglazed off-white porcelain—in 1839. But after the Civil War, the great pottery-makers swarmed into the Pennsylvania-Ohio pottery belt, and by the turn of the century such entrepreneurs as Isaac Knowles and William Bloor were turning out more pottery than any other area of the world.

Some of the great names in American china have vanished into history. The names of Castleton, Franciscan, Flintridge, and Syracuse no longer appear as backstamps. Gorham (in California), Pickard (in Illinois) and Lenox (in New Jersey) still manufacture fine china. Most other producers buy imported porcelains and apply the decoration locally.

The Shape of Things to Come

A century ago, a potter would naturally position his factory near his sources of supply. Proximity of kaolin deposits meant the springing up of porcelain houses. Today, hauling bags of kaolin from Georgia to Illinois or Arizona adds an inconsequential cost. The porcelain-maker can locate where he or she chooses.

But the industry has an international flavor today. A producer thinks nothing of preparing transfers in Italy, firing plate "blanks" in Japan, and decorating the plate and adding gold bands and numbers in Newcastle, Pennsylvania.

We live in an age of specialization, and indications are that platemaking will become more specialized over the next few decades.

Is this good? For the collector, probably. A producer can sift through suppliers, demanding and getting the best quality and price regardless of geography. The producer isn't limited by a single platemaker's capabilities, equipment, or formulations.

Take a look at some of your plates. Who made them? Where were they actually fired—as "blanks" and as finished plates? Who made the transfers?

No matter. You're part of a great and wonderful tradition in ceramic art. Enjoy it, and look forward to more of the same!

Chapter 2

The Not-So-Natural History of Plate Collecting

The most famous advertisement in the history of plate collecting is exactly four inches long. The headline:

"WOMAN FINDS $1,500 DISH IN ATTIC"

This ad first appeared in 1975, the brainchild of J. Roderick ("Rod") MacArthur. MacArthur was the founder and owner of the Bradford Exchange, and until his death in 1984 he was the principal spokesman, the prime mover, and far and away the most important trend-setter in plate collecting.

(The dish the woman "found" was the 1965 Lalique crystal plate called *Deux Oiseaux*—"Two Birds." Issued at $25, the plate shot up in value on Bradford's "Bradex listings" of traded value until it showed a listed worth of $1,500. While an increase of 6000% was certainly atypical of the plate market, it was a lovely idea for an ad.)

The ad no longer runs, and coincidentally the 1965 Lalique plate no longer is worth $1,500. It lists for $1,000 but regularly sells for less. Part of the reason, unquestionably, is that Lalique ended the series suddenly, after issuing the twelfth annual crystal plate in 1976.

Pre-Bradford Plate Collecting

Before Bradford, plate collecting was neither organized nor profitable. The Danish porcelain house, Bing & Grøndahl, started it all with a little Copenhagen Blue plate called *Behind the Frozen Window*, in 1895. Intended as a Christmas gift for lesser friends and servants, the plate sold for about 50 cents.

That it now sells for more than $3,200 is less surprising than the realization that so many of these historic plates still exist. It's a tribute to the beauty and eternal molecular structure of hard-paste porcelain.

Bing & Grøndahl has issued a Christmas plate every year since 1895, including the difficult 1939-1945 war years.

In 1908 another famous Danish porcelain house, Royal Copenhagen, began issuing Christmas plates. Rosenthal of Germany joined the Christmas plate-makers in 1910. The Dutch company Royal Delft began issuing its 10″ Christmas plate in 1915. (The 1915 Royal Delft plate, called *Christmas Bells*, has traditionally been the most expensive "back issue," selling for $6,000 to $7,000.)

That was pretty much the story until 1968 and 1969, when somehow a whole group of platemakers sensed that the volcano of public demand was about to erupt.

In 1967 the German company Bareuther issued a Christmas plate, beginning a series that continues unbroken. The following year Porsgrund, a Norwegian company, issued its first Christmas plate (the Porsgrund series ended in 1977). Also in 1968, Rorstrand of Sweden issued the first of its still-ongoing series of Christmas plates.

But 1969 was the seminal year for contemporary plate collecting. In that year, Bing & Grøndahl again broke fresh ground by issuing the first Mother's Day plate, *Dog and Puppies*. Wedgwood issued its first Christmas plate, *Windsor Castle*. The combination of a new reason for plate-issuance—Mother's Day—and a Jasperware collector's plate seemed to trigger the planning process in many another platemaker.

By 1971, when Goebel issued the first of its Hummel plates and Gorham started two separate trends with its first set of Norman Rockwell *Four Seasons* plates, all that was missing was a catalyst that would set the rocket engines in action.

(Gorham's two "firsts": 1) The first widely-distributed collector's plates in full color; 2) the first plates not tied to an event such as Christmas or Mother's Day.)

Bradford: The Catalyst

J. Roderick MacArthur was the son of John Mac-Arthur, founder of Bankers Life & Casualty Company and one of the two or three wealthiest tycoons in America.

The relationship between father and son was stormy. Rod MacArthur worked for a time at Citizens Bank, a Chicago financial institution controlled by his father. By 1972, when he took over a corporate shell called Bradford Galleries Exchange, Ltd., his father was living in semi-retirement in Palm Beach, Florida.

In 1973, Bradford originated the *Bradex,* an organized listing of plates and their "latest trading prices."

Obviously, in 1973 only a handful of pioneers were in the plate business. One was Hollywood Limited Editions, operated by William Freudenberg Senior and Junior, in Chicago; another was Viking Import House, operated by Patricia Owen, which had opened its doors in 1949 in Fort Lauderdale. A third, and Bradford's principal competitor for years, was Joy's Limited Editions, run by James Petrozzini.

In 1975, following a dispute with his father, Rod MacArthur renamed the company The Bradford Exchange, Ltd.

Over the years Bradford's influence in plate collecting has been profound. Bradford alumni are in key positions with many leading producers; the company's listings of plate values have outlived "Plate

Price Trends," published in the now-defunct *Plate Collector* magazine.

The MacArthur family owns *Plate World* magazine. The company, or surviving members of the MacArthur family, are principals of the Edwin M. Knowles China Company. They also have an interest in D'Arceau-Limoges, Limoges-Turgot, Konigszelt-Bayern, and other brand names familiar to most collectors.

The 1983 Crash and All That

For years, producing plates paralleled laying golden eggs. It seemed no producer could make a mistake. Retail collectibles shops sprang up in every shopping mall, and major producers began issuing plates at a clip that kept plate "blank" manufacturers in Europe, Japan, and the United States working overtime.

"Continuity programs" appeared—series of six, eight, a dozen plates issued at monthly intervals. Collectors were bombarded. Instead of choosing between two Copenhagen Blue Christmas plates, collectors could, if they had the money, buy 700 to 1200 plates a year and still not have a complete collection.

Then momentum slowed.

Between 1983 and 1986, many dealers closed their doors or shifted to giftware. Numerous mail order companies quietly dropped from the scene. Publications went out of business, for want of subscribers and advertisers. Producers, some of them highly regarded, vanished.

But by 1987 the drought was ending. Dealers once again—however cautiously—were buying inventory. Bing & Grøndahl and Royal Copenhagen consolidated their U.S. operations, adding stability and power to the two most venerable names in the world of plate collecting.

And for the Future...

The future of plate collecting isn't in the hands of those of us who already collect plates.

The future of plate collecting seems well assured because the world of plates transcends any generation gap. Those in their 20s, 30s, and 40s are as avid as those in their 50s and 60s. As we approach the 1990s we see the appeal broadening even further, with plates whose themes are aimed at infants and youngsters. (See "Priming the Next Generation" in chapter 12.)

What makes most plate prognosticators enthusiastic about the future is the interest members of every age group seem to be developing—plus the broadening of plate subject matter beyond cute children, fuzzy animals, flowers, and birds.

As plate collecting sophisticates itself, some of the earlier experiments may be repeated. During the golden days of the mid-1970s, producers introduced plates with art by Pablo Picasso, Salvador Dali, and LeRoy Neiman. They all bombed.

Plate collectors have been attuned to the art of Norman Rockwell and Edna Hibel. Probably the 1970s, when most collectors were in their 50s and 60s, was too soon to test contemporary art on plates.

The 1990s? Wait and see.

Chapter 3

All About Backstamps

You always can tell if your dinner guests are plate collectors:

If they surreptitiously turn over their dinner plates to look at the backstamp, they're part of our Porcelain Underground.

To a serious collector the backstamp is as much a key to the plate's worth and authenticity as the motif on the front. In fact, in some cases the backstamp is *more* important than the images on the face.

For example, the *Massachusetts Mutual Rockwells* are Norman Rockwell sketches (*Baby's First Step, Little Shaver, Happy "Berthday" Dear Mother*) which the insurance company who commissioned the art has made available to all comers. Result? Lots of plates, by different producers, with identical art.

What makes one plate different from another isn't the image on the face but the backstamp.

Do They Buy the Plate— or the Backstamp?

Visualize any collector—or yourself—in a retail store.

"This registration number is smudged!"

"What's this blue squiggle under the printed plate title?"

"Last year's plate had a backstamp printed in brown. This year's is in black. What's wrong?"

"The number goes over the wording around it. Give me a different plate."

These are the same collectors who shrug at the uneven application of the bold border or a speck in the porcelain itself. The face of the plate may be subject to human frailties, but we won't tolerate imperfection in the backstamp.

What's In a Backstamp?

The venerable giants of limited edition plates have relatively simple backstamps.

Bing & Grøndahl, progenitor of us all, has as a backstamp for its annual Christmas plate the traditional B&G three-tower symbol, ringed by the words "Copenhagen Porcelain Made in Denmark." Below is an issue number (not necessarily in sequence: the

1975 Mother's Day plate has the number 9375; the 1975 Christmas plate has 9073) and the plate title in Danish and in English, without quotation marks. Royal Copenhagen's annual Danish blue Christmas plate has the Royal Copenhagen name ringing the crown symbol, the wavy-line RC symbol, perhaps a set of initials hand-scribed (probably the individual decorator's parallel to "Inspected by No. 17" in a suit of clothes), and the title, again in Danish and English.

Both these backstamps are restrained and unobtrusive, using only a couple of inches of the area within the plate's footrim. Compare them to this legend on a plate:

"Swan Lake"
by
Robert Clarke
Plate V
of a series of six
limited-edition plates
in the series
"Dance, Ballerina, Dance!"
an edition limited to
14,500 worldwide
of which this is plate
number 27
produced by
Kaiser Porzellanfabrik
(Kaiser logo)
KAISER
W. Germany
for
The International Museum
(Museum logo)
c MCMLXXXII, MIM

This backstamp copy fills the footrim, a diameter of about four inches.

The maximum information a backstamp can hold depends on external factors: The issuer of the plate, whether the artist is featured, whether the plate has a pre-announced edition limit, whether the plate is numbered, whether the plate is part of a series, and on occasion whether the face of the plate is decorated with lead-free colors or not.

Before explaining this last point, let's explore the rest of it. Some plates have no apparent issuer. They're either premiums or stock items, or the issuer prefers for one reason or another to be anonymous.

Today, in an era of artist-glorification, backstamps tend to include not only the artist's name but the signature, even though the identical signature may appear on the plate face. The traditional Danish plates didn't and don't mention the artist, although the name is no secret; the Danish blues are of a pattern, and continuity is stronger if the individual remains in the background, artisan rather than artist, working within a pre-established format.

As collectors know, editions can be limited in four ways—year of issue, number of orders received, firing days, and absolute pre-announced limit. Usually, the backstamp reflects the edition limit only in the last instance, although a copyright or issue line (if not on the face of the plate) mentions the year of issue.

If the plate is numbered, obviously the number appears on the backstamp. The plate serial number can be hand applied or machine printed.

A backstamp, even one which appears to be hand lettered, is a screen-printed transfer on lacquer-covered paper. A window die-cut into the lacquer is the hole in which the plate decorator scribes the plate number. If this is done with a gold pen, the backstamp is fired as the plate's gold rim (if any) is fired.

Today, plates are available with a pre-gilded rim. Scribing the number on the backstamp would mean a special firing just for the number; so the producer has backstamp transfers made with a numbering machine automatically advancing the individual number with each printed backstamp.

It's easy to tell the difference: The pre-numbered backstamps *look* printed. Even though they're neater and less trouble to apply, they can generate a different kind of trouble of their own: If one is damaged, that number is lost, and a hot-selling series may require a special reprint of backstamps with random fill-in numbers.

Don't Eat Tomatoes On Your Rockwells

For a while, in the late 1970s, plate producers were including a printed admonition on some backstamps. It read something like this:

PLEASE OBSERVE:
This plate is for decorative
purposes only. In order to
create the unique coloration

and effects, special heavy
metallic ceramic pigments were
used for the design. These
pigments can cause lead or
cadmium poisoning if used for
the service of food.

Sometimes the caution was worded more gingerly, but the meaning was: We didn't use lead-free and cadmium-free pigments, as we would for dinnerware. Why? Because lead-free colors aren't as vivid as colors with lead, and for a collector's plate a vivid image is more important than being able to eat foods whose acids might release those colors (foods like tomatoes).

Custom Backstamps

Every now and then a producer will custom-fire a collector's name right into the backstamp.

D'Arceau-Limoges did this with the pioneer *Lafayette Legacy* series, as an extra "heritage" plate to the series. Veneto Flair did it with some of their handcrafted Christmas plates.

This is a mixed bag. All of us like the notion of having our names immortalized on our plates, but sometimes, when customized plates are presented for sale, the owner has a difficult time finding a buyer. Who wants a plate with a stranger's name on it?

So customized backstamps make sense as family heirlooms. They're a questionable blessing as investments.

(One irreverent note: It's possible with a "gold eraser" to remove gold from a plate, even when the gold has been fired into the backstamp. Gold erasers aren't for casual use, though, because rubbing too hard can scratch the plate.)

A Temporary Conclusion

At this writing, backstamps are in a period of temporary retrenchment.

According to the transfer houses specializing in backstamps, some producers are taking the economy route—standard colors instead of gold, limited use of art, and reduced space to enable the transfer house to get more backstamps on a printed sheet.

Backstamps reflect trends in plate collecting, and this current situation suggests a period of conservatism.

But plate collecting is a dynamic, changing world. What collectors want, collectors get, and lavish backstamps have been the cause of too many impulse buys by collectors to fall into a total decline.

To us, the ideal backstamp combines validation of the plate's pedigree with the true spirit of collecting—*exclusivity in fine art.*

So keep turning those plates over, folks. If you only look at the face and ignore the back, you're missing half the fun.

Chapter 4

Whose Art Is It, Anyway?

(A Look at Plate Art Styles)

An art museum is a wonderful place for a plate collector to develop an inferiority complex.

Wandering through the galleries, we hear mini-lectures:

> "He's the acknowledged master of romantic impressionism."

> "Her neoclassicism is tempered by illustrative realism."

> "Obviously, his cubistic period evolved into neoprimitivism."

Who wouldn't feel cowed in that minefield of term-throwers?

Art, like music and literature, is peopled by two groups: Those who study it clinically, and those who love it emotionally. Sometimes an individual will belong to both groups, but not often. Plate collectors, thank goodness, usually belong to the second group ...and this may explain why plates have become the most collected art form in the world.

This chapter will be your easy guide through the minefield. We aren't suggesting you'd want to compete with the term-throwers and name-droppers; we do think good taste is more important than a label.

The Two Styles of Art

For the purpose of clarification, let's divide plate art into two "families": *Representational* and *nonrepresentational*.

We don't want to be term-throwers ourselves, so a logical definition of the difference between the two might be this: Representational art is supposed to look like the subject the artist is painting, and the key is instant recognizability. Within this family of art styles is a wide range of art techniques.

Nonrepresentational art is an emotion-based or intellect-based image of what the subject means to the artist.

Confused? Don't be. We'll give you some examples to light the path. Anyway, at least 80 percent of all plate art is representational, so it's probably more important to sub-categorize types of representational art than to give the two art families equal space.

Types of Representational Art

First, a disclaimer: This isn't an art textbook; it's a plate collector's handbook. If you want an eight-year course in fine art, this isn't it. Rather, this is a plate collecting basic.

We sub-classify representational art into five main "schools," and we'll suggest plenty of plate examples for each school:

1. Photorealism

2. Impressionism

3. Combined photorealism and impressionism

4. Romanticism

5. Illustration

The words should suggest the art styles subscribing to these schools. All are representational, because all these artists intend their art to look like the subjects they're painting.

Photorealistic Art

You don't have to guess to understand this type of art. It's a painting which depicts the subject the way a camera would photograph it, as accurately and as detailed as possible.

Want some examples of this art style? Here are five:

- *Courtship Flight,* by Mario Fernandez (Pickard)
- *Dark Eyes,* by Jay Schmidt (Kern Collectibles)
- *Children of Aberdeen,* by Kee Fung Ng (Artists of the World)
- *American Rose* series, by Luther Bookout (American Rose Society)
- *American Panther,* by James Lockhart (Pickard)

The discipline of the photorealistic artist is restraint: He resists the temptation to embellish or exaggerate. The subject looks exactly as it does in life.

Impressionistic Art

Impressionism was introduced as an art style by French artists who tried to capture the effect (or "impression") of sunlight. Rather than blending their colors they painted bold strokes of pure color, to trick the eye into seeing the *impression* the sun might give.

Technically, impressionists usually display bold brush strokes, often textured.

Some examples of impressionism in collector's plates:

- *Joanna and Jon,* by Addie Heesen Cooper (Bing & Gróndahl)
- *Storytime,* by MaGo (Royal Doulton)
- *Marie-Ange,* by Paul Durand (Limoges-Turgot)

Each of these artists visualizes the effect of *light*

on the subject. Instead of painting a smooth photographic image, they concentrate on the color impression light creates.

A good test for impressionism: Stand back a few feet and squint. The picture will seem to be more sharply focused.

Combination Photorealistic and Impressionistic Art

The best of both possible worlds? Devoted fans of Francisco Masseria think so!

Masseria's art combines the discipline and detail of photorealism with the light effects of impressionism. The faces of his subjects sometimes inspire collectors to look, look, look—is it a painting or a photograph?

Clothing, hair, and background are areas in which Masseria's broad brush strokes and lavish use of color make him an exponent of this hybrid school of art.

A Masseria example: *Gabriella* (Royal Doulton).

Romantic Art

Romanticism is a cousin of impressionism. The romanticists, like the impressionists, don't paint exactly what they see. Rather, they paint a "romanticized" image.

The result combines the smooth technique of the old masters, enhanced with the interplay of light and shadow.

Some examples of romantic art:

- *Jason and Ginger*, by Peter Fromme-Douglas (Anna Perenna)
- *Feeding Time*, by Thornton Utz (Viletta)
- *Once Upon a Time*, by Sandra Kuck (Reco)
- *Lilies of the Field*, by Pati Bannister (Schmid)

You can see the breadth of romanticism—from the porcelain smoothness of Fromme-Douglas to the broad brush strokes of Utz.

The quality which brings these artists together as "romantics" is the deliberate and thoughtful technique: Painting their subjects realistically, but leading the viewer to see more than would be there for a photographer. . .or for us, if we looked at their subjects through our own eyes instead of theirs.

Illustrator or Fine Artist?

Norman Rockwell was surely the most beloved artist of this century, and his art is better known, more recognizable, and more imitated than any other artist who ever put brush to canvas.

Why is it, then, that one can look in vain

through books with titles such as *Biographies of Great Artists* and never see Rockwell's name, nor the name of his mentor, Joseph C. Leyendecker?

To the purists, the gap between fine artist and illustrator parallels the gap in fashion between hand-stitched and machine-made. The word "illustrator" suggests a "for-hire" artist instead of one who creates "from the soul."

Our opinion: Malarkey. But please: Qualify that as our opinion. There are no facts in art appreciation.

No question about it: Most of Norman Rockwell's paintings were the result of someone commissioning him to paint a specific—a *Saturday Evening Post* cover, or an ad for Mazda light bulbs, or a sketch for Massachusetts Mutual Insurance Company. Rockwell's commercial success stemmed from the same nucleus that generated his position as the giant of collectible art: The difference between illustration and photorealistic art.

Photorealism or Illustration?
There IS a Difference

Illustration differs from photorealism in the way the artist depicts the subject. The illustrator exaggerates some specifics slightly, to add emphasis. The design of the motif makes the point.

An illustrator can carry his art deep into the *un*realistic, maintaining the illustrative style. The result very well could be a scene that can't exist, painted with photographic fidelity as though it did exist.

Oh, yes, Rockwell *could* paint in a photorealistic way. His *Four Freedoms* and *The Golden Rule* prove how easily he moved across the fine line border. But his illustrations, especially those reflecting his wry sense of humor, are the paintings most collectors seek out. Why? Because when he *wasn't* being realistic he was being wry—emphasizing a human foible, bringing a smile to a situation. Collectors love it.

Some plate art by contemporary illustrators:

- *DeGrazia and the Mountain*, by Larry Toschik (Artists of the World)

- *Music for a Queen*, by Lynn Lupetti (Dave Grossman Designs)

- *Morning Glow*, by Alan Murray (Ernst)

Types of Nonrepresentational Art

We'll risk being called simplistic by the occasional reader who may be curator of a major museum. We've categorized nonrepresentational art into six categories:

1. Stylistic
2. Design
3. Cartoon
4. Abstract expressionism

5. Provincial/primitive

6. Surrealism

The gulf between the various categories is like the gulf between two bodies of land. Sometimes it's as wide as a sea and sometimes it's as narrow as a river. For instance, you might think no relationship exists between surrealism and cartoons, but the common threads are many. And stylized art is a first cousin to cartoons, a brother to design and primitivism, and a sister to both abstract expressionism and surrealism.

Nonrepresentational art accounts for only about 20 percent of plate art. Why? Because some collectors are uncomfortable with pictures that don't look like life itself, pictures that seem to be closer to Bugs Bunny than Michelangelo, or pictures whose message is abstruse enough to demand close examination bordering on study.

Stylistic Art

Stylized art makes no attempt to give lifelike qualities to the subject. Important elements are separated, isolated, and exaggerated; all else is reduced to background or eliminated altogether. The painting, then, gains its drama from the emphasis that comes from exaggeration.

A few examples of stylized plate art:

- *Los Niños*, by Ted DeGrazia (Gorham)

- *Mary and Jesus*, by Eve Licea (Knowles)

- *Serenity*, by Berta Hummel (Schmid)

- *Clowns and Unicorns*, by Margaret Kane (Anna-Perenna)

Design Art

Here's where a description gets tricky!

The difference between stylized art and design isn't always clear cut. The easiest way to tell them apart is that stylized art regards shapes and colors as more important than the subjects they represent.

The design-artist extracts just the lines and colors he or she regards as the keys to the image. In a sense, design is the art of subtraction. Colors are never blended, as they might be in stylized art.

Thus, a stylized bowl of flowers still is a recognizable bowl of flowers; you may have to turn on your imagination to recognize it as a bowl of flowers when it's painted as a design. (Another identity problem: Design can lap over into cartoon.)

Some examples of design plate art:

- *The Baptism of Christ*, by Bjorn Wiinblad (Rosenthal)

- The Santa Clara plates from Spain (artist undisclosed), especially the 1970 and 1978 issues

- *The Holly and the Ivy*, by Gillian West (Spode)

Cartoon Art

Oddly, cartoons are in a sense representational because they depict an actual subject in a recognizable manner.

But there is where any relationship with representational art ends. The cartoonist keeps only the design of the subject, reduced to its simplest form. Colors are simple and bright.

The very nature of a cartoon is amusement. We can't visualize a serious message transmitted by a cartoon (although many military training films use cartoon characters such as Mickey Mouse to simplify the instruction).

Some examples of cartoon art:

- *Freddie the Freeloader,* by Red Skelton (Fairmont)
- *Filling the Stocking,* by Charles Schulz (Schmid)
- *Woody Woodpecker,* by Walter Lantz (Armstrong)

Abstract Expressionism

Abstract expressionism—a terrifying term, isn't it?

Be of good cheer. Abstract expressionism terrifies most art critics, too. Sometimes they don't know whether to applaud a painting or burn it, because the artist exercises total control: "It's a bird because I say it's a bird."

The abstract expressionist carries his view of a subject well beyond the design stage, and may even (as in Picasso's art) create a completely unrecognizable image. He "abstracts" the most basic elements and "expresses" the spirit he sees.

Examples of abstract expressionism:

- Picasso plates issued in 1976 (Jack Childers)
- *Pierrot*, by LeRoy Neiman (Royal Doulton)

Provincial/Primitive Art

Innocent simplicity is the key to primitive art. We aren't supposed to believe the image actually looks like the subject, but we have no difficulty deciding what that subject is.

Colors are pure and bright; the design is elemental. The effect is childlike—sometimes the kind of art a child might paint. This is one reason primitive art is so popular for Holiday greeting cards.

The word "provincial" enters the mix because so much of this art has a country or provincial subject.

Examples of provincial/primitive art:

- *Hallowe'en*, by Grandma Moses (Royal Cornwall)
- *Lemminkainen's Chase*, by Raija Uosikkinen (Arabia)
- *The Adoration*, by Heidi Keller (Koenigselt Bavaria)

Surrealism

The last category of nonrepresentational art is surrealism. This art is the greatest challenge to both artist and viewer.

Successful surrealistic art can haunt the viewer's mind for days, because the emotional wallop is so powerful; unsuccessful surrealism can turn on the viewer's rejection as no other type of art can.

Surrealism uses fantastic or incongruous imagery, painted in a highly *realistic* manner. The effect is an idea depicted in its extreme. This form of art can ridicule or extol; it can glorify or denigrate. What power a talented surrealist has!

Some examples of surrealistic plate art:

- *Gold Bean*, by Salvadore Dali (Rosenthal)
- *Mother and Child*, by Ole Winther (Hutschenreuther)

Conclusion

One of the more charming characteristics of the typical plate collector is that unlike some gallery-goers who like to show off how many arty words they know, the collector buys what he or she likes and doesn't care what the style is called.

Never change, dear collectors. Your attitude is what keeps plate collecting inside the real world, a mirror of actual tastes and likes, far from the strutting and posing and phoniness that infests so much of the art world today.

The background we've supplied in this chapter is just that—background. Don't let us or anyone tell you what you're supposed to collect.

Chapter 5

The Mechanics of
Platemaking

About 30,000 years ago Tumac the Caveman dropped his clay dish into the fire at the mouth of his cave. He was annoyed, because he had baked his dish in the sun for two days to finish it.

Tumac said the caveman-equivalent of, "My beautiful dish is ruined."

He was wrong. When he was able to fish his dish out of the fire, he found a couple of improvements he inadvertently had added: His dish no longer absorbed (and leaked) water. It no longer became mushy when he put something hot into it. And it didn't disappear into a mud pie during a pelting rain as its sun-fired brethren did.

Far more than Harald Bing, Tumac became the father of plate collecting. But he would be astounded at the variations of his discovery available today— and, like many collectors, he might be confused by some of the interchangeable terminology.

A Guide Through the Mystic Maze of Terms

The word pottery usually means earthenware: Opaque, porous clay. A flowerpot qualifies as earthenware, just as many of the inexpensive decorative pieces around your home do—and perhaps your everyday dishes.

Porcelain differs from pottery in a number of ways, all of which add expense to its manufacture and all of which add significance to the collector. The key to porcelain is a special clay, kaolin. The clay is named after Kaoling, China, where it first was found; in the United States, pockets of kaolin clay exist in Georgia, South Carolina, and Utah; major kaolin deposits have been found in Great Britain, France, Germany, India, Japan, Czechoslovakia, Austria, and Russia.

The kaolin gives porcelain its hardness, but another ingredient gives it the translucency we associate with fine porcelain. We'll get to that.

Naturally, porcelain production has centered around the kaolin-producing areas. Decomposed feldspar is what separates kaolin from ordinary clays; it's the only clay that can hold its shape without warping at the inferno-hot kiln temperatures at which the clay-mix becomes porcelain. Kaolin gives porcelain its classic cool white body.

But wait, you say. I have some pure porcelain

pieces, and they're cream-colored.

Yes and no.

If your pieces are genuine porcelain, which "ping" with a high clear note when you tap the edge with a pencil, what you have is a blend developed in the Far East in an attempt to match American china, which is cream colored.

The technique is as simple as adding a tinted background to a painting. As the clay mixture is being turned into paste, before being given its plate shape, a pigment is added. On firing, the pigment changes the original white color to cream.

Anyone who knows what to look for can spot the difference between cream-tinted porcelain and cream-toned American china in two seconds. But if most of the plate face is covered with art, the difference is inconsequential to most collectors.

Porcelain's translucency comes from another ingredient, one less well-known than kaolin: Petuntse (pronounced puh-toont-seh). Kaolin is partially decomposed feldspar; petuntse is partially decomposed granite.

The principal difference between porcelain and earthenware is in its *vitrification*—a molecular change into a hard, glassy substance.

The change is the result of intense heat. Porcelain is fired at temperatures hotter than 1350 degrees celsius. That makes it tough. An unvitrified or semi-vitrified dish may shatter when dropped on the floor, but a porcelain dish may survive—and dent the floor.

Is China Porcelain?
Is Porcelain China?

Because hard-paste porcelain originated in China, we often say "china" when we mean "porcelain," and vice versa.

China does have porcelain clays as principal ingredients: Petuntse and kaolin are the keys, except for bone china. But there's a technical difference: China plates are fired at temperatures about 10 percent cooler than hard-paste porcelain.

Even that isn't the biggest difference. If you're making a porcelain plate you have a glaze firing, in which the glaze literally permeates the plate body, even hotter than the original firing. For china, the glaze firing is at a lower temperature than the original firing, which means the glaze *doesn't* permeate the plate body.

In the United States no company makes porcelain plates, and of a once-thriving china industry only three are left: Gorham, Pickard, and Lenox.

If no one in the United States makes porcelain plates, where do they come from?

Most of the collector's plates are on "blanks" imported from Japan, France, or Germany. The transfers are applied and fired into the plates by decorating shops in this country.

In recent years, additional contenders have begun to ship porcelain blanks to the United States for decorating. Brazil, Israel, Taiwan, India, and mainland China are after the highly competitive U.S. market for the porcelain plates on which collectible themes will appear after firing in American kilns.

Bone china? The formulation differs. Around 1800, an English potter named Josiah Spode changed his china mixture to include the ash of burned animal bones. When he increased the bone ash content to 40 percent or more of the total mix, he found he'd produced a warm, creamy hard-paste china which retained its durability even when spun into dishes of unusual thinness. The translucency was superior, too.

Spode left his name on the industry; Spode China still exists, a division of Royal Worcester. Bone china is still a popular medium for dinnerware as well as collector's plates.

The Overlooked Giant: Stoneware

Because stoneware usually is heavy and less delicate-looking than porcelain or fine china, collectors often have an unreasonable contempt for this member of the plate family.

They shouldn't. Unlike earthenware, stoneware is fully vitrified. If you break a stoneware plate, you can see from the edge that it's glassy throughout, just as porcelain is. It won't absorb liquid through the broken edge.

The main difference between stoneware and

porcelain is the original group of clays in the formulation. They aren't as highly refined as porcelain clays, and the result in production is that they can't hold their shape when formed into thin bodies—they sag and buckle.

If a platemaker fires stoneware clays at the ultra-high temperatures he uses to make porcelain, the plate literally "melts."

Still, stoneware is strong and serviceable; if the ball-clay is white, the plate will be white, and the difference between good stoneware and porcelain isn't as clear cut as the difference between the color red and the color green.

American stoneware history has lots of names we still see on the table: Homer Laughlin, Buffalo China, and Syracuse China are a few. As you can tell from the familiar names, you see stoneware plates most often as hotel china.

Now That You Know the Difference...

If you want to attach any significance to this short course in china, our suggestion is:

Go back to square one, the litany you've heard since you first started collecting plates:

Buy a plate because you like it, not because you're in awe of the production method.

But then...

Don't buy a plate that's out-of-round, warped, or misshapen. You'll be apologizing for it instead of boasting about it, and very soon you *won't* have a plate you like but one you wish you'd never bought. (That's what chapter 6 is all about, so keep reading.) Whether your plate goes "ping!" or "clunk!" when you tap it, if it looks good, has a crisp image, and matches the advertising claims by the producer, you have a winner.

Chapter 6

When Is a Plate Defective,
and What Can You Do
About It?

==========

You've just opened the sealed box, to have a first look at your newest plate treasure. Then you look at the backstamp. Uh-oh. You turn the plate back and forth. The backstamp doesn't line up with the face of the plate.

A touchstone for this reference was an experience we ourselves had: A plate we had helped develop finally came. We affixed a permanent plate-hanger to the back, squarely centered above the backstamp. When we hung the plate, it was skewed to one side.

That wasn't surprising. What *was* surprising was the reaction we had from several plate producers who felt we were being arbitrary and picky when we wrote in a magazine article that a misaligned backstamp is unacceptable in plate production.

We stand our ground about lining up the backstamp, but the question of what is and isn't a defective plate has become a controversial issue, with collectors exercising their *caveat emptor* right of finicky rejection and producers pleading for collector-education to prevent the return of perfectly good plates.

In the course of writing this chapter, we interviewed manufacturers, distributors, dealers, and collectors. Comments ranged from the quip by one of the largest and best-known producers (who asked for anonymity), "If it leaks, then it's defective," to the almost religious catechism, "There's no such thing as a perfect plate."

All parties agree that collectors are becoming more knowledgeable about their hobby. Why is this so? They meet at local clubs and compare not just notes on their collections, but actual plates from the same edition. They attend plate conventions. They see films and hear lectures. And they read.

Defective Colors? Maybe.

The art on the face of the plate is the number one area of inspection by producer and collector alike. It also is the number one source of collector rejection.

The motive is easy to examine, which is why so many collectors, whose objection to their acquisition may be that they simply decided they shouldn't have bought the plate in the first place, invent a reason for returning it. More logically, they claim, "The plate doesn't match the picture in the sales literature."

Ceramic plates use metallic pigments which burst into the full range of the palette only when they are fired at carefully controlled temperatures—usually between 1375 and 1425 degrees Fahrenheit. Collectors who compare their plates with others fired at the same time have become adept at spotting differences in tint and hue.

Five degrees of difference in the kiln can make a difference in color intensity. These variations are a natural result of the firing process and are *not* defects. Since heat rises, the same kiln-load could have a 10 degree differential from the top of the kiln to the bottom, and subtle color changes from plate to plate are what you'd expect. These variations are acceptable. They aren't rejects.

But—

Reds are the quickest colors to "fire out." This means that reds are most likely to burn away. Visualize this: A plate with a lot of reds in it is stacked at the very top of the kiln, where temperatures are hottest. Even as the bottom plates are firing to a brilliant red, the top ones go through their optimum coloration and burn to a faded brown-gray.

Every manufacturer and decorator has several inspection-stations, but inspectors become hypnotized by the sameness of what they're viewing. The deterioration from red to blah *isn't* an acceptable variation; that plate is defective, and if you know your clown's putty-colored nose should be fire-engine bright, you have a defective plate. Ask for a replacement.

A Picture Isn't Worth a Thousand (returned) Plates

Dealer after dealer comments on collectors who walk in with a magazine or mailer showing a plate in full color. They see the plate, compare it with the printed piece, and walk out, convinced they've avoided an insidious plot to hoodwink them.

This attitude problem stems from comparing printing inks, which are transparent, with ceramic pigments, which are opaque. But it isn't the collector's fault. He or she saw a picture, and all the collector wants is for the plate to look like the picture.

No, it's the producer's fault if that paper reproduction was made from the original art and not from the plate itself. It's perfectly normal to do that, and for new issues it's as common as breathing; that doesn't make it right. (See chapter 10, "Plate Advertising.")

More important: It doesn't make the plate defective.

The proofing process requires months and months. The transfer house says, "We'll have proofs by such-and-such a date." Now the producer begins his advertising campaign. He knows he'll have plates, but he doesn't have them yet.

What does he do? He photographs the art from which the plate will be made (and perhaps strips that "color separation" into a blank gold-banded plate, if his plate has such a rim). If he isn't familiar with the characteristics of metallic fire-on pigments, he may complain to the transfer house, as the collector later complains to him: "The transfer doesn't look exactly like the art."

Nor can it.

Sometimes an artist who really understands porcelain as a medium for art will know how specific colors fire relative to each other—which colors literally "eat" the colors around them, which ones combine in strange ways, which are bold and which retreat. His original art may, in fact, look underpainted. Ah, but when that plate is fired, the porcelain gives the art a luminescence, a pearl-like quality no other type of art can match.

This becomes a classic issue, a perfect marriage of art and technology. The plate is far superior to the printed descriptive piece. It's different—but it's *better*. Defective? Of course not.

(Collectors who make a point of the difference between the printed picture of a plate and its actual appearance often single out the Hutschenreuther *Enchantment* series which featured the art of Dolores Valenza. On the cover of each box was a picture of the plate inside that box. The box was printed; the plate was fired. The plate isn't as brilliantly colored as the picture on the box; it glows with its own gentle radiance. Yet, because it differs, some regard it as defective.)

The rule of coloration might be:

> *Judge the art on a plate on its own merits, not in comparison with a printed reproduction.*

The Good, the Bad, and the Ugly

Splotches of "foreign" colors are a different matter. If you see black specks in a blue sky, or brown moles on what's supposed to be a flawless complexion, that plate is defective. The transfer should have been scrapped before application to the plate.

What happens in the offset lithography process is that despite some of the most sophisticated cleaning and dust-removal equipment you'll find in any lithography plant, specks remain after one color has been laid down, and those specks attach themselves, wherever they fall, when the next color goes down. If the rollers haven't been cleaned thoroughly, a tiny splotch may appear regularly in one area. If six transfers are made on a single sheet, one of those six will be affected, which means if the transfer-run is 6,000 pictures, 1,000 will have that spot.

Uh-huh. If your plate has that problem, not only did the original inspector in the transfer house goof; so did whoever checked the sheets at the decorating facility, where the transfers were put onto the plate. So did whoever checked the finished plates.

Send yours back.

Oddly, if that same inspector erroneously passes a plate whose porcelain or china body is defective, it's less likely a collector or a dealer will send it back as defective. In a sense, it's a healthy indicator: Importance is centered where it should be, on the picture.

Sloppiness, though, is a no-no. Everyone whose fortunes or pleasures come from plate collecting should remember the advantage plates have over books, tapestries, or oil paintings: A plate can last almost forever, and when you accept a plate with pronounced warpage or visible iron particles, you're helping immortalize a mistake.

"Let Me Tell You About My Aberration"

Let's start at the beginning, expanding on a point from the previous chapter:

The clay in your plate is usually either American china clay from Georgia or West Virginia or bone china from England, fired at very hot temperatures, or porcelain "kaolin" clay from Bavaria, France, Brazil, or Japan, fired at somewhat lower temperatures. Both the china and the porcelain bodies undergo a second "glaze" firing—a lower temperature for porcelain, and an extremely hot firing for the china glaze.

All clays shrink by about 15 percent during the firing processes. Because ceramic clays are flexible in their wet stage, this plasticity and shrinkage means some variation in the final shape and size. A plate advertised as 9″ may be 8³/4″ or 9¹/4″. *It's not defective.*

Extreme warpage is a different matter. No two plates will have the exact same degree of "dish," but they should all be acceptably round and well-shaped.

You can see the acceptable variations of shape by observing any stack of fine dinnerware in your cupboard—the space between the plates can vary considerably, but each is acceptable individually.

Unacceptable warpage means a plate sags to one side; its footrim is uneven; the entire *coupe* curve collapses into a flat saucer.

Such aberrations are so obvious they seldom reach the marketplace. But if you put your plate face up on a flat table and the plate won't rest evenly on its footrim, then sit so you face the plate edge-on and slowly rotate it. You may see that one side is higher than the other. Our opinion: A little wobble is unimportant; if your plate has a pronounced lopsided look, ask for another.

It Ain't Necessarily So

We enjoy pointing out to guests in our home, who question the differences in the shapes of their plates, a stack of twelve of the very finest and most expensive Limoges dinnerware in our china cabinet.

In the stack, the space between plates ranges from 1/4″ to 5/8″. Many are somewhere in between. This obviously is because some of the plates have a flatter "dish" than others. Believe us, if we thought this made them defective, the manufacturer would hear from us. They aren't, and he won't. They're the best there is, and we know, as you should know, if they were absolutely identical they'd be so machine-made we couldn't regard them as fine porcelain.

(Because of the higher initial firing temperatures, American china and bone china are less likely to have variations in dish-depth than porcelain. If you have dinnerware of several types, stack some dishes and check for yourself.)

Henry "Pete" Pickard, head of much-honored Pickard China, typifies responsible producer attitude in his comment to us:

"I'm pleased to see collectors becoming more knowledgeable about what they should expect in plate quality; but they should appreciate the fact that no manufacturer, not even Pickard, can make a 'perfect' plate."

If you see a brown or black spot on the back of an ivory plate, chances are it's iron oxide. That you can see it with the unaided eye means the plate is a "second." Send it back.

A chip in the footrim? Defective. A rough, jagged spot on the edge? Defective. Blisters where the air wasn't forced out when the transfer fired on? Defective.

Collectors sometimes invent defects because they don't know how the plate is *supposed* to look. A collector who bought a lovely cloisonné plate, made in the Orient, asked us to look at the tiny pinholes in the colored enamel on the face of the plate. "Isn't this defective?" she asked us.

We reassured her. One test of true cloisonné enamel is these pinholes. The enamel is finely-ground glass powder which melts and flows during the firing process. It bubbles, leaving minute craters in the surface as it cools. If you have a totally smooth cloisonné piece, chances are it's made with an enamel *paint* applied directly to the plate without firing; it isn't real cloisonné at all.

Maintain Your Perspective

Pat Owen, owner of Viking Import House, a major distributor and dealer of collectibles, who has been in the business for nearly forty years, offers sage counsel:

"Maintain your perspective. Don't apply the standards you use for a $200 plate to judge a $19.50 plate."

Mrs. Owen points out that the same individual who immediately recognizes the difference between a Hyundai and an El Dorado or between an inexpensive dress and a designer original may lose perspective when a $19.50 plate isn't as thin as a $200 plate, or has fewer colors.

Another large-volume dealer, Marge Rosenberg of Carol's Gift Shop in Artesia, California, told us she asks all her customers to look at a collector's plate the way they'd view any work of art:

"I say to my customer, 'Please stand back while I hold the plate for you. View it as you would an oil painting. Your plate is man-made and can never be perfect.' "

Mrs. Rosenberg also reminds her customer-collectors to expect the best possible plate within each price range but not to confuse the resources available to the producer of a $25 plate with those within reach of the issuer of a $100 plate. In her store, each plate is inspected before being added to inventory. She rejects rough edges and surfaces. But she cautions against "dissecting an object of beauty."

Manufacturers, producers, and distributors ask dealers to share their education with their collectors. Apparently, though, many dealers fear collector wrath and will open every boxed plate of a motif if a customer wants to pick one out. Of the many films and books about collector's plates, not one deals with what appears to be a touchy issue.

Do dealers themselves make unreasonable claims of imperfection? Some producers think they do. "I believe it's because of the uncertain economic times," said one. "We're suddenly getting back plates with a note saying they're imperfect. They aren't. In fact, we ship them out to another store. What's happened is the dealer can't pay for them and doesn't want to admit it. Proof? The dealer who returns good plates claiming they're faulty doesn't want replacement; that dealer wants a credit on the account. We understand it, but we don't appreciate it."

The Enlightened Collector

Almost universally, executives of plate producing distributing and retailing companies agree that an enlightened collector is the best collector. He or she knows what's possible and what isn't, what's a defect and what's a natural variation, what's important as art and what's an insignificant difference in coloration. Capricious complaints are exasperating, but no responsible plate producer wants an imperfect plate carrying his name to perdition forever.

To the collector who doesn't quite know what we mean, we suggest a visit to the Louvre. A small painting hangs on one wall. Other works of art are larger. Others have bigger, brighter frames. This painting shows cracks in the varnish—a defect, surely? Yet nothing in the most famous art museum on earth compares with the Mona Lisa.

A visit such as that tends to put our sense of what's important in perspective.

Chapter 7

Series Length:
How Many Is Enough?

How many days in *The Twelve Days of Christmas?* Twelve, right?

Wrong.

You forgot about the *Jubilee* plate. Twelve regular plates plus one extra plate makes thirteen.

Series length has become a puzzling and seldom-answered question for producers of limited edition plates. Three coexisting and mutually exclusive philosophies exist:

1. Since the words "First Edition" have magic in plates, a short series—four plates, for example—can be ended quickly, enabling the producer to re-start with a new "First Edition" of what in fact is a second cycle—a retread.

2. Since many companies selling continuity series by mail feel it's as easy to market an eight-plate series as a six-plate series, it falls to reason it will be as easy to market a twelve-plate series as an eight-plate series. So closed-end series gravitate toward the twelve plate length.

3. With very few exceptions such as the Lalique Annual and the Bethlehem Christmas plate, those who issue "event" plates (Mother's Day, Christmas) or annuals feel with logical justification that their plates should follow the pattern set by Bing & Gróndahl nearly ninety years ago—let it go on forever, building momentum or propelled by its own hard core of prior collectors.

The "Endless" Series

We ourselves have had discussions with three producers about an endless subscription series. In each case, the sales literature would emphasize the "cosmic" nature of the series. Plates would be interchangeable, not identified as "Plate II" or "Ninth Issue." Coherence would come from allocating matched registration numbers to subscribers. Possible? Logistically, yes. Probable? We'd guess that someone will try this within the next decade, and we hope (as serious collectors always hope) it won't be a producer who pays more attention to being different and offering "flash" than to bringing a valuable addition to the world of limited edition plates.

What about the non-series—the single plate that was *supposed* to start a series, then stood alone as the producer ran out of money or decided to quit after issuing the first plate?

Collectors who complain bitterly about being left with an "orphan" plate should take another look, not only at the plate but at their motives.

Suppose, for example, someone begins a series called *Rudolph the Red-Nosed Reindeer*. The theme will parallel the story of the song. Out comes plate number one, showing Rudolph with his shiny, glowing nose. Some collectors say, "Oh, boy!" and clamor for the second plate; too many others yawn and say, "Another cutesie-pie Christmas plate." The first plate is the only one ever issued.

Our opinion: So what? If the plate brings cheer to the home...if the owner doesn't have to give a six-page explanation to anyone who views it (a problem with people who collect for the wrong reason)...if the collector hasn't prepaid for merchandise not delivered...then that collector has a temporary annoyance caused by the producer's overambition or cynicism, but there's no permanent damage.

Collectors who fear this possibility should recognize that although their fears aren't ridiculous, so far no *major* plate producer has abandoned a series in mid-issue, even though in a number of cases the latter plates have been unprofitable. Minor producers? Take your best hold.

"Four Seasons"—Unassailable Marketing Logic

What *is* logical as a series length? Back in 1971, Gorham began a profitable tradition: The annual Rockwell *Four Seasons* set, issued together. The first *Four Seasons* showed a profit for collectors as well as for the producer, with an original issue price of $50 and a current value of $220 (it has been listed as high as $495).

Four Seasons plates have been an unassailable way of quadrupling the number of plates a producer offers to collectors at one time, or within one year. A chickadee represents winter; a robin represents spring; a hummingbird represents summer; a lonely seagull represents autumn. Or, an evergreen is winter; a crocus is spring; a rose is summer; a colorful group of leaves is autumn. Voila! Four seasons: Four plates marketed with the effort and advertising expense of selling one.

The Cost of Advertising: Prime Motivator

Advertising expense has been the motivator of many continuity series sold by mail, and our opinion is this has benefited the collectors who bought those plates. Why? Because if the producer were to circularize collectors for each plate separately, the project might be self-defeating: The cost of mailings and constant regeneration of a collector-base would push up the cost of the plates—which would cut the number of eligible and interested collectors, which would lower the number of plates made, which would push the cost even higher, which would...

One maxim is etched deep into the brains of producers:

Collectors demand completeness.

Translated into marketing, this means a solid percentage (averaging 40 percent to 60 percent) of those who collect Plate I of a six-plate series will loyally pay their way through Plate VI. From the producer's point of view, the profit/loss aspect is unassailable. He knows:

> 1. He will sell more than one-sixth the number of single plates he would sell if he offered the collector only one plate.
>
> 2. Charge card buyers continue uninterrupted unless, as is true of book and record clubs, they make a positive move to cancel. (This technique of shipping until the buyer requests cancellation is called "negative option.")
>
> 3. Cash buyers are likely to continue because collectors demand completeness.
>
> 4. The break-even point is far below the break-even point for a single plate.

Note that these points are far more true of companies selling by mail than conventional retail stores. Retailers tend to be unenthusiastic about any continuity series with an interval of only a few months between plates, because to their customers the act of buying is a more visible process than that of the mail-order buyer. Too, a retailer, whose stock is comprised of plates from many sources and whose clientele changes from day to day, finds it difficult to establish an order-pattern for six plates tumbling out of what seems to be an endless mill at the rate of one every other month. What happens if that retailer sells out of Plate III and then finds a customer who wants all six?

The Most Popular Length: Six Plates

At this writing, six plates seems to be the most popular length for a *closed-end* plate series (i.e., a series which pre-announces the number of motifs). The first big-selling series of this length is also the most famous continuity series of all time, one which most observers agree launched modern plate collecting: The *Lafayette Legacy* collection, six plates issued by the Bradford Exchange between 1973 and 1976 (plus one extra plate with the subscriber's name fired into the backstamp, issued as an option to those who had acquired the complete series).

D'Arceau-Limoges also issued the first twelve-plate continuity series, *Women of the Century*, between 1976 and 1979. Production difficulties caused the unusually long issue period for this series, which was marketed only by mail; no plates went to dealers.

Since *Women of the Century*, various producers have issued at least two dozen twelve-plate series with subjects ranging from the Old Testament to flowers. Several have been successful enough to warrant follow-up with a *second* twelve-plate series. Invariably, nearly half the subscribers of a "sequel" series are those who already have the first.

Although the most popular current length for a continuity series is six plates, eight-plate series are whittling away at this lead. A producer who has made the change from six-plate programs to eight-plate programs put it this way:

"The six-plate decision often is made out a neatness complex—a plate every other month for one year. But eight plates are as easy a 'collection' concept to sell to a collector as six, and the theme is more thoroughly developed. Oh, yes, and the financial aspect is better by light-years."

Don't Tell an Artist, "Drop Dead." It Could Happen

What happens if the artist quits or drops dead in the middle of a series? It happened to Bradford's introductory series from Limoges-Turgot. Paul Durand completed only four paintings for the series *Les Enfants de Durand* before his untimely death. The series ended with the issuance of the fourth plate.

Leo Jansen and Ted deGrazia had only one-plate-at-a-time issues when they died. Death isn't the only series-shortener: Artists are artists, and they can have a "snit-fit" or an argument over royalties. We know of two such circumstances in which the artist threatened to stop painting future motifs unless royalties were increased.

These potential problems have led to caution. But while most producers will wait for completion of all the paintings of a *Four Seasons* series before advertising, this isn't universally true of producers who have dollars tied up in six- to twelve-plate series, especially when the artist doesn't have Norman Rockwell's speed (some plate artists labor over a single original for four to six months).

The producer will mail a brochure which glorifies Plate I, the all-powerful first edition; it also may show Plates II and III. Then, clever graphic treatment covers the absence of additional pictures, or a photographer shoots a picture of twelve plates in a hutch cabinet from a distance, making positive identification of each motif impossible.

Sometimes the result of advertising a series before all the paintings are ready is bizarre. We ourselves once worked on such a series in which after the titles had been announced, the artist absolutely, positively was unable to paint a respectable image of the eighth subject. After months of frustration on all sides, the subject was changed, and later mailings reflected this change. As we recall, only half a dozen collectors ever commented on the change, and of that half dozen only two or three objected.

On another occasion "proofing" difficulties with the third of twelve plates would have caused a two-month delay. The fourth plate was ready, and the mailing company switched the sequence, with a short enclosure-note explaining why the switch was made.

Of about 10,000 collectors who got that note, as far as we know not one cancelled the series.

Why didn't more collectors object? Series collectors want completeness, so they'll accept an inferior plate within the series even though they don't like the art. This is a big advantage series producers have over single plate producers, who initiate their reputations afresh each year: A less-effective piece of art can be buried within the series.

As you might expect, the big drop-off in a continuity series is between the first and second plates. Knowing this, a producer sometimes will offer as the *second* plate the most attractive motif of a series, assuming that the first plate can carry itself just by *being* a first edition.

Once past the second plate hurdle, a series sails along serenely with few dropouts. In fact, some collectors get itchy if a later plate in the series is delayed; they write reminder letters asking the issuing company if they've been overlooked or forgotten.

And for the 1990s. . .

An evolution of the late-1980s seems to be the issuance of several series of plates, by the same artist, simultaneously. In one instance, as collectors were getting their first look at the first edition of a series of clowns, the same company issued a new series of plates by the same artist, featuring—clowns!

Another artist has Indian princesses, Indian

chiefs, and Indians on horseback, all different series and all marketed at the same time.

While not objectionable from a collector's point of view and actually admirable from a marketing point of view, this type of *intensification process* can lead to confusion in the collector marketplace parallel to the chaos caused by some conflicting Rockwell plates.

What will the next few years bring?

In our opinion, the economics of continuity series are unassailable.

As individual companies compile lists of collectors, what could be more sensible than catering to those collectors' demand for completeness with a subscription series?

(If one of those series is planned to go on forever, we'll let you know.)

Chapter 8

How to Sell or
Trade Your Plates

Ask a collector: "What if you had to sell your collection? What would you do?"

Two-to-one the answer would be, "I'd put an ad in the paper."

Ask the same collector: "What if you want to trade some plates?"

Two-to-one the answer would be, "I'd go to a Swap 'n' Sell at a plate convention."

Both these answers are logical. But they aren't the only answers. In this chapter we'll take a look at six separate ways of turning over your collection, or any part of it.

Method No. 1:
Local Newspaper Ads

Newspapers as an advertising medium haven't changed in hundreds of years. But recognition of plates as an art form has changed even during the past 10 years.

One major change: It's commonplace today for a collector to advertise plates as fine art, at prices far above a plate's issue price. Even a few years ago if you'd advertised an 1895 Bing & Grøndahl Christmas plate for $500—about one-eighth its actual market value—only a handful of experienced collectors would have bid on it. Try that today and your phone will ring off the wall.

Let's not kid ourselves: Knowledgeable collectors won't pay an inflated price. They know as well as we do where to get a particular plate on the secondary market, and they can read the *Bradex* just as we can.

But if you advertise a plate at what to you seems to be an unrealistically high price, outsiders, who have heard of plate price appreciation but not experienced it, just might respond to your ad. (Logically, you're better off setting your own price level with lesser-known plates than with market leaders whose resale value has been established elsewhere.)

Don't be upset if a prospective buyer says you've overpriced a plate. You only need one buyer...and you always can drop the price.

Which brings us to two tips:

a) Get the names and phone numbers of anyone who answers your ad, whether he or she buys or not. These people are the nucleus of your next sale, or of the closeouts of whatever you have left after the weekend; and they can be the start of your own enterprise, a point we'll discuss later on.

b) If you have a whole list of plates, buy a one-inch or

two-inch display ad in the main news section instead of a classified ad. People who never look at the classifieds will be exposed to your ad.

Method No. 2: Collector Publication Ads

This method has changed because several of the publications have gone out of business.

We won't suggest any magazines, because we'd be accused of professional prejudice if we left one out; but be sure, before wasting postage and time, the magazine in which you want to advertise accepts such ads. Some don't.

Consider, in running an ad in a national publication: When you make a sale you'll have to wrap and ship the plate, taking a risk of breakage. For the individual, collector publication ads are "iffy" at this time.

Method No. 3: The Bradford Exchange

Bradford matches buyers and sellers, and the disintegration of Method No. 2 has made Bradford a popular outlet.

But don't expect overnight action unless you happen to get lucky and offer a plate on which the Exchange has no backlog, just when a buyer is at hand.

Bradford charges a sales commission and usually won't handle plates not listed on the Bradex. That *excludes* thousands of plates. So be sure you understand all the rules before giving a listing to Bradford.

A tip: Nothing prevents you from listing your plate with Bradford and trying to sell it yourself at the same time. If you sell it first, just withdraw your listing.

Method No. 4: Swap 'n' Sells and Method No. 5: Plate clubs

These aren't the powerhouse methods they used to be because we don't have as many Swap 'n' Sells as we used to, and clubs are less active. Yes, the South Bend Show still rockets along, but some of the regional shows don't have the attendance or the wallop they did in the pre-1983 years.

Local clubs still have Swap 'n' Sells, but right now there seem to be a lot more sellers than buyers. This may be because some of the early movers and shakers, who brought local clubs to full flower in the 1975-1984 decade, have begun to step down; a new generation of dynamic leaders hasn't yet been welded into place.

A tip: Why not make some phone calls and put

together your own Swap 'n' Sell? It's fun, it's sociable, and it can be profitable for you.

Method No. 6:
Selling to a Dealer

In our opinion this method is the one that has changed most in the past few years.

Dealers never were enthusiastic about buying plates, except from their regular customers. Today, show up at a dealer with a handful of plates and be ready for an insultingly low offer.

Two reasons for this: First, a dealer can sit with a back issue for months or even years. Ultimately the dealer will include your plate with a bunch of others at bargain prices. Even then it might not sell.

Second, the 1988 dealer implicitly prefers to sell new issues. These are promoted by the producers, and they're easier to sell, especially to a new customer. The dealer doesn't have to explain the entire theory of plate collecting, as he'd have to do when showing a vintage plate.

A tip: Approach a dealer with a trade-in, not an outright sale. Use the plates you no longer want as partial payment on new plates you're buying. Most dealers welcome this type of transaction. But be careful—it's like trading your car on a new model. You can wind up paying full price for a plate every dealer is discounting, which means your "trade-in" hasn't brought you anything.

So much for conventional techniques. Is anything new?

Yes, depending on your own interest.

The key is the second half of the subhead of this chapter: "How to Sell *or Trade* Your Plates." Swap 'n' Sells aside, you can have a merry time trading plates, and yes, you can make a profit doing it.

How can you make money when no dollars change hands? It's a paper profit, to be sure, but at the end, when you have a garage sale or run your ad in the local paper, you'll come out ahead.

Here's how it works: You literally form your own club. Start a list of every local collector you can find. When you have a dozen or more, send them a note telling them you're starting a local plate-trading group (*not* a club). Ask them to list, on a form you provide, all the plates they'd like to swap or sell.

Most folks are lazy. Follow up with a phone call and take down the plate availabilities over the phone.

Then make one more mailing—the various availabilities—to all the people who have responded. That's only fair.

But you're one step ahead. Call with an offer to swap plates, for those you want.

Be sure to have a value-reference at hand when initiating a trade. If you're a knowledgeable trader you'll come out ahead, because most collectors decide to part with a plate because it no longer excites them; the value of the plate is secondary.

So you'll exchange your "tired" plates for a new batch, and because you're the one who has suggested the trade, you'll come out ahead on the resale value of the plates.

Why bother? Because you won't spend that much time, you'll have some fun, and you'll meet some people who probably are worth knowing. And oh, yes—you'll have some new plates, worth more than the ones you traded.

Here's the ultimate point: The plate secondary market isn't what it used to be, and opportunities for aggressive selling and trading are dramatically reduced from the golden days of the late 1970s and early 1980s.

It's up to collectors to make their own marketplace. Obviously, trading is easier than selling; obviously, it's easier to sell at a top price to a new collector than to an old-timer; obviously, patience pays; and obviously, if your original purpose in collecting was to acquire plates you like, you can be selective when trying to place those plates in a new home.

Chapter 9

Edition Limits:
A New Look at
an Old Controversy

The controversy continues: What, logically, determines an edition limit?

Note, please, that we said *logically*—not *legally*. This isn't an issue we expect to see tested in a court case; the test, rather, is in the hands of collectors who decide to buy a plate based on a multitude of emotional, artistic, and financial considerations—with "edition limit" as one component of the mix.

The Four Ways to Limit an Edition

Historically, producers have limited editions in one of four ways:

1. Year of issue.

This is where it all started, with the Copenhagen

Blue Christmas plates. Bing & Gróndahl issued *Behind the Frozen Window* for the Christmas season, 1895; the company hasn't ever changed its edition limit from year of issue; each Christmas plate is shown at various trade shows in January and is issued for that year. The edition limit is a specified terminal date, unrelated to a specific number of plates.

B&G imposes this same limitation technique on its Mother's Day plate. Royal Copenhagen, similarly, limits its editions by year of issue, as do most issuers of holiday-related annuals. Some name a terminal day ("Firing will cease December 24, 1988") but most make no promotional point of this limitation. Producers usually don't number annual plates, and many don't include a certificate of authenticity (the certificate is a refinement which didn't become common until the 1970s).

2. Collector equivalence.

Some plate historians call this the "Franklin Mint" limitation, after the company that popularized it (but no longer uses it): "The number of plates produced will be exactly equivalent to the number of reservations received."

Plates using the collector equivalence limitation usually have numbers and certificates. Purists sometimes object that this limitation is no limitation at all, since the producer is free to make all the plates he can sell; but certainly collector equivalence qualifies as a valid limitation technique. The point is moot these days, since no producer we know of currently uses it.

3. Firing days.

This is the most controversial of plate limitation techniques. Opponents say it suggests a limit that isn't really there, since a) firing days needn't be consecutive, and b) a producer can farm a hot-selling plate out to a number of plate decorators whose combined daily capacity then becomes astronomical. Plates may or may not be numbered; numbering sometimes combines code initials with the numerical digits.

As we'll explain in a moment, the objection isn't itself completely logical in light of the universal concept of plate collecting; one can justify either the "pro" or "con" viewpoint toward firing days.

4. Absolute limitation.

This is the easiest edition-limiting procedure to understand. The producer announces, as he introduces a plate, a specified edition limit: 5,000 plates, or 10,000 plates, or 19,500 plates, or whatever. This limit is absolute. The producer might make fewer plates but not more. Usually, plates are numbered sequentially, without code initials.

Expensive plates gravitate toward this fourth technique, since it suggests exclusivity.

There's a fifth approach, universally condemned by established members of the plate collecting world.

Producers, dealers, and veteran collectors alike express annoyance at what we might call the "Declarative Limitation"—the producer simply declares, "This is a strictly limited edition," without ever explaining how it's limited.

The Yeas and Nays

Let's explore the three current limitation techniques—year of issue, firing days, and absolute limitation.

We'll skip equivalence and declaration because equivalence is out of fashion and true collectors—those who are reading this book—probably aren't logical targets for the borderline producers who give only a declaration—lip service—to edition limits.

Year of issue seems to be a limitation with which everyone is comfortable. This probably is because year of issue is the most venerable of all limitations and because so many of the best-known producers use it.

We hear few arguments about year of issue because we never see producer abuse and because the technique matches the type of issue. It makes perfect sense for an annual plate to be issued during the year of issue, especially when the year itself may be part of the art-motif.

The firing-day limitation isn't universally revered, but it's considerably less debatable than it was when producers first popularized it in the late 1970s.

One reason for increased acceptance is that so many of the most popular plate issues carry this type of edition limit. As we pointed out before, the edition limit is only one facet of the promotional mix, and as we'll point out a little later on, most collectors who want a plate ask only that there be *some* kind of limitation.

Absolute limit is, of course, beyond reproach. What isn't beyond reproach is the occasional advertising campaign glorifying edition limit beyond any other attraction the plate might have for collectors.

Newcomers to plate collecting have no problem understanding an absolute limitation: "When these are spoken for, there won't be any more." They can be bewildered by firing days, not only because they don't know what a firing day is but also because they have no frame of reference. A typical question: "If it takes about eight hours to fire a plate, does that mean a company can fire only three plates a day?"

Proof of this confusion is an episode in mid-1987 in which a collector registered a formal complaint with the Better Business Bureau about the ethics of the Hamilton Collection, of Jacksonville, Florida.

As reported in *Advertising Age*, the collector said he had bought a plate—*Mr. Spock*—in 1984, assuming the edition was limited by an announced number of firing days. Some years later, Hamilton still was advertising the plate.

Hamilton's rejoinder was standard: Nothing in the advertising stated *consecutive* firing days.

So we still have only a partial answer to the limitation enigma. The ultimate resolution lies squarely in the hands of—you guessed it!—you, the collector, the irrefutable authority, the moment-of-truth critic.

Let's share some opinions from various sides of the table. We'll tell you in advance: The diversity of opinions tells us we're far from a universal solution.

Here's What They Say

Collector viewpoint is discouraging, because it reflects a Pollyanna approach, a wonderful world that cannot be:

"Why don't all the producers get together and agree on one kind of plate limit—and then all issue plates that way?"

Why don't they? Because whenever you get more than one plate producer in a room, you'll have an argument. Producers range from tiny boutiques to enormous corporate giants.

But that isn't the major problem with this simplistic solution. If all plates cost $100 and had a 7,500 edition limit, the laws of economics would make possible this standard limit; but they don't have a standard look and limit, and all of us hope they won't.

In fact, if the mechanical aspects of collector's plates were standardized, every plate would be 9″ in diameter, have a gold band, and come in a gray styrofoam box. What a dull world we'd have! And how quickly we'd kill off plate collecting, by regimenting it and forcing it into a too-tight uniform!

A reasonable approach is typified by Eloise Parks, former president of the National Association of Limited Edition Dealers and head of Eloise's Collectibles, Houston. Says Ms. Parks:

"In my years of listening to collectors, and watching the successes and failures of limited edition plates, I've come to the conclusion that although some collectors care deeply about the size of an edition, many others don't care at all.

"The artist, the subject matter, the use of pleasing colors, the reputation of the producer—all these factors seem to be more important than edition size. I've seen many very-limited plates and series which haven't been popular with collectors. Similarly, many plates and series with unannounced limits and with limits set by firing days have become runaway successes with demand far exceeding supply."

A less enthusiastic comment comes from a dealer who says:

"Sure, the best-selling plates to existing collectors seem to be those with a 'firing-days' limit. But a firing-days limit makes no sense to new collectors we're trying to recruit. The producer's ads make it seem glamorous, but *we* have to explain it."

Sam Polk, past president of the Collector Platemakers Guild and head of the producing company Collectors International (whose plates are fired by Royal Doulton), is an outspoken critic of firing days. Mr. Polk made this comment to us:

"The more information a producer can give the buyer, the more confidence the buyer will have in the validity of the producer. Royal Doulton has always believed the practice of limiting any edition by the number of firing days has no real significance. As they have stated publicly, if Doulton limited any issue to 30 firing days, this could easily give them enough time in their vast production facilities to create more than 3,000,000 of any given plate.

"Those plates listed as annuals and issued during a specified calendar year, and those with announced edition limits, are the only legitimate methods of keeping faith with the buying public on the question of limited edition collectibles."

The United States president of the "patriarch" plate producer, Paul Steffensen of the now-combined U.S. operations of Royal Copenhagen and Bing & Grøndahl, takes a paternal view toward all types of plate limitation. Says Mr. Steffensen:

"Bing & Grøndahl issues two types of limited edition plates—those with a pre-announced edition size, such as our *Christmas in America*, limited to 15,000 plates; and those such as our Christmas plate, limited to the calendar year of issue. Both are absolutely limited. For plates available throughout the year of issue, on December 31 of that year all molds are destroyed.

"But I would like to think that collectors, who have so many plates from which to choose, make their decision based on what they see on the face of the plate."

We'd like to see that too, Mr. Steffensen.

Our Viewpoint Is Valid

Digging into the background of the limitation question, and discussing it with some industry leaders, convinces us once again that our original viewpoint still is valid:

Buy a plate because you like it. Buy it because you intend to hang it on your wall or display it with pride in your *étagère*. Buy it because it has a theme or art style you admire.

If the edition limit coincides with your personal philosophy, that's the frosting on the cake.

Ask us in the year 2001 to report on the state of edition limits again. We'll bet the comments would be the same.

Chapter 10

Plate Advertising:
What to Believe and
What to Doubt

All plate collectors can be divided into two categories:

1. Those who know what they want.
2. Those who don't know what they want.

The second group of collectors—those who don't know what they want—can be divided into two categories:

1. Those who believe plate advertising.
2. Those who don't believe plate advertising.

Each of these two subgroups has a quality we admire. Those who believe plate advertising are the reason plate producers work so hard creating imaginative motifs and imaginative advertising campaigns. They're the reason the world of plate collecting has advanced to where it is today.

Those who don't believe plate advertising keep everyone honest. Although they probably extend their innate suspicions to include advertising for automobiles, beer, and fast-food restaurants (which isn't a bad idea for all of us), they're the governor on what otherwise might be a runaway express with no sane hand at the throttle.

Honest or Dishonest Claims?

It may surprise you to learn that by standards of 99.44 percent purity, many plate ads might be considered dishonest.

For example, a producer might be planning to issue a new plate three months from now. The art has been approved, and he is in the final stages of "proofing." He knows he'll have plates, so any claims he might make relative to availability probably will be true.

But here's his problem: He wants to announce his plate coincidentally with first availability of that plate.

Do you see the dilemma? You do, if you've read chapter 6.

Right now, he doesn't have plates. All he has is a color transparency of the original art. The closing date for his magazine advertising is at hand. What does he do?

Right! He uses that transparency of the original art as the illustration in his ad.

Hold it, you say. That can't be right. The plate has a gold rim, and the picture in the magazine shows it with a gold rim. It *must* be a picture of the plate, not the original art.

Every color separator knows how to do this. The picture of the art is "stripped into" a photograph of a blank plate with a gold rim. The result: a handsome color illustration of what appears to be the finished plate.

The questions is, *should the reader react negatively to this practice?*

In our opinion, no.

We say this not only because it's so widespread, but also for a technical reason.

Did you ever try to photograph one of your plates? Try it. You'll find it almost impossible to shoot that plate without having an obliterating glare on the face of it.

Suppose the producer did shoot the plate itself. He might get that same glare, and when you looked at the picture you'd think the glare is a permanent part of the motif. That's farther from the truth than shooting the original art.

(Actually, you *can* eliminate the glare by shooting the plate inside a tent made of white nylon, using your lights to illuminate the nylon rather than the plate. The result is a soft, even, glare-free light. But who wants to go through all that?)

When *should* you rise up in outraged wrath? When the photograph, it turns out, bears no resemblance to the finished plate. Here's a gorgeous, colorful, dynamic picture in the magazine; the finished plate is washed-out, pale and out-of-register. That's a dishonest ad claim, even though not one written word is the source of guilt.

The Selective Use of Facts

If you're in the advertising business, you're used to the question, "Why doesn't anybody believe advertising any more?"

The answer is as artless as the question: "Because so much advertising crosses over the unguarded border separating self-glorification from hogwash."

The world of plates is especially vulnerable to claims that have little to do with the inherent worth of the plate but much to do with the inability of the advertising writer to present a compelling sales pitch. It's a shame: Fifty years ago we'd have believed statements we now routinely reject.

Know why? We're a television-trained society. Television, that magnificent sophisticator, regularly gives us (supposedly for evaluation) identical claims by direct competitors, spaced barely fifteen minutes apart. We come to the conclusion that since all detergents make the same claim, probably all of them are lying; since all automobiles claim the best value and the best ride, and since all seem to be filmed in a murky, wet, smoke-filled garage, all but one of them are lying. When competitors make parallel claims, the result is confusion—which in turn breeds skepticism.

Then, when we read plate advertising, part of

our implicit skepticism (the doubt bred by television) affects our reaction. For plate advertising to be believable, that advertising should avoid these common pitfalls—gaps in logic which sooner or later are a turn-off for collectors:

Pitfall No. 1: The Interchangeable Claim

The number one reason for disbelieving plate advertising is formula writing—making a claim we've seen a hundred times before and have quit believing long before spotting this ad or opening this piece of mail. Some examples of the Interchangeable Claim:

> "We searched for the one artist capable of portraying this theme and are proud to announce that the noted artist [NAME] is creating his/her first plate series."

> "Plate 'Firsts' from [TYPE OF ARTIST] Earn Top-Dollar Market Appreciation."

> "A spectacular limited edition, created exclusively by renowned artist [NAME]."

Pitfall No. 2: The Touchstone Lie

This pitfall is subtler than the Interchangeable Claim. The Touchstone Lie is a falsehood based on an unrelated truth.

The collectibles advertiser who uses this device is cunning rather than clever. The target of the advertising message may accept the lie; feel uncomfortable without knowing why; or reject the message. Certainly we're not a nation of careful readers. Some collectibles publications rent their list of subscriber names 40 to 60 times a year, to companies selling collectibles by mail. The readers of these publications, obviously the most dedicated of all collectors, are bombarded with competing sales messages from a multiplicity of sources. How can they evaluate any particular offer with care?

So some companies establish a policy of the Touchstone Lie and use it as formula writing. Every offer begins something like this:

> "No event is as important to a knowledgeable collector as the first announcement of a major new collection by one of the world's foremost names in collectible art. Such an occurrence is rare and eagerly anticipated by the world of art and collectibles alike..."

What is this cataclysmic event? A company which issues half a dozen series a year is announcing its *First Ever Owl Collection.*

Another example of the Touchstone Lie:

> "As a first edition, this plate has even more significance. It joins the elite group of plates known as 'classics.' Here are just a few examples of some first editions and their performance in the secondary market:
>
> 1965 Lalique Annual issued at $25, rose in listed value to $1700.

1971 Goebel Hummel issued at $25, rose in listed value to $1200..."

Can you see the pattern in the Touchstone Lie? The foundation is true. It's a fact. *Yes*, the first announcement by a major company is an important event to collectors. *Yes*, the classic first editions have done well in the secondary market, although current values are lower. The advertiser uses these as touchstones, riding their coattails because they exist, not because his offer qualifies to join the magic circle.

Pitfall No. 3:
The Anonymous Endorsement

An ad begins:

"Absolutely irresistable...Positively Utz!"

We didn't furnish the quotation marks; the advertiser did. What he didn't furnish was the name of someone who said that. Was it Mrs. Utz? A collector? A dealer? Or the person who wrote the ad?

(There's also a spelling error: It's "irresistible," not "irresistable.")

We're fans of Utz and think his plates have warmth and style. For the producer to share this view is natural; for the producer to cheat by suggesting that an *internal* piece of advertising puffery originated at an *outside* source also is natural, but it's cheating.

Another example of the Anonymous Endorsement:

> "One dealer said, 'I can't keep these plates in stock. They fly out the door as fast as they fly in.' "

A purist would attack the use of plurals. A limited edition sells best when the collector feels he's one of a chosen handful, not one of the mob: "I can't keep this plate in stock" surely is preferable to "I can't keep these plates in stock." That isn't the question, though. The question is, who *is* this dealer? If a dealer is willing to be quoted, why does he want to be anonymous?

Conclusion: This isn't a dealer talking; it's the ad writer.

Pitfall No. 4:
The Standard Cliché

How many ads and mailed offers have you read that have these words and phrases in them?

> "Frozen in time..."
>
> "Captured forever in the eternal medium of porcelain..."
>
> "Immortalized for all time to come..." (a redundancy)
>
> "One of the greatest artists of all time..."
>
> "Buy now and save..."

The plate that started it all: *Behind the Frozen Window* by Bing and Grøndahl, issued in 1895 for the equivalent of 50¢, began a Christmas series of blue and white, relief porcelain plates that remains unbroken. The plate has sold for as much as $4,000. An astonishing number still exist.

"Stylized" has pictorial components carefully arranged by the artist to stage the subject as part of the total design. Individual elements are less important than the total design effect. Charlotte and William Hallett painted this stylized design for Hutschenreuther.

Impressionism—the artist's attempt to portray the effects of sunlight—is a popular art style for plate art. Kaiser's *Lilie* by Gerda Neubacher shows us why.

Country Fair by Sickbert, for the Franklin Mint, is an example of naive or primitive art. Bright colors and simple figures give it a child-like quality.

Clowns have always been one of the most popular—and financially safe—themes for collector's plates. The ongoing success of clown motifs reflects the truism that all collectors enjoy happy subjects.

Venerable comedian Red Skelton paints his own happy character "Freddy the Freeloader" for collector's plates, preserving his innocent harmless humor in the permanence of porcelain.

Small children and cuddly animals are two "never miss" subjects for plate art. Often they're combined, as Thornton Utz did in *Best Friends* for the Hamilton Collection.

Should the producer have put the words of the "Now I Lay Me Down to Sleep" prayer on the face of this plate instead of on the backstamp? The typical collector says, "No!", although logic probably says, "Yes." To the collector, the backstamp is the plate's pedigree.

Orchard Mother and Child by Juan Ferrandiz for ANRI uses special lighting effects to create the idealized concept of madonna and child. The romanticism is heightened by the exaggerated youth of the mother.

Dominic Mingolla is an artist who works in enamel-on-copper.
This collector's plate was issued by Calhoun's Collectors Society.

Bing & Gröndahl created another first—the first annual collector's plate commemorating an event or holiday other than Christmas. In 1969, B&G began its annual Mother's Day series with this plate, *Dog and Puppies*. The words "Mors Dag" mean "Mother's Day" in Danish.

This Hummel Christmas plate features art by "Berta Hummel" and is issued by Schmid. Another Hummel Christmas plate series uses art by "Sister Maria Innocentia Hummel" and is issued by Goebel. The dispute between the two companies over rights to Hummel art was finally resolved in the mid-1980s.

Hand-thrown terra cotta clay is used to form the individually-made earthenware plates by Tiziano for Italy's Veneto Flair. The coarse red clay is fired at relatively low temperatures and retains its porosity.

Wedgwood's Jasperware is far better known than is their true porcelain; but these relief plates are made from unglazed stoneware. An example is the Wedgwood 1981 Christmas plate, *Marble Arch*.

Ten Lords A'Leaping, the 1979 Christmas plate from Haviland of Limoges, France, is one example of the popular collector's plate theme of Christmas carols. Spode of Great Britain, Kaiser of Germany, and several other plate producers also have used Christmas carols as plate subjects.

Fairy tales are popular sources of inspiration for plate makers
from many countries. Villeroy and Boch's Mettlach plate shows
their version of *Snow White and the Seven Dwarfs.*

Vague Shadows of the United States issued a series of fairy tale
plates, using paintings by Gregory Perillo. Shown here is *Little
Red Riding Hood.*

Haviland Porcelain of Limoges, France, produced a series of fairy tale plates with scenes from *The Arabian Nights.*

Heinrich of Germany issued a series of fairy tale plates illustrating Russian fairy tales. This one is titled *The Snow Maiden at the Court of Tsar Berendei.*

Children's books inspire many plate series. Pictured here is *The Queen's Croquet Match* from the *Alice in Wonderland* series painted for Royal Cornwall by Lawrence Whittaker. At least two other producers have issued *Alice in Wonderland* plates.

"Cinnabar"—carved, red lacquerware—exemplifies exotic non-porcelain collector's plates. This plate, *Sense of Touch,* is one of a series issued by Royal Cornwall titled *The Five Perceptions of Weo Cho.*

"Chokin" is the generic name of an etched metal plate, highlighted with gold and silver. This one was issued by the Hamilton Collection.

The words "Not intended for food use" are an admonition based on the use of colors whose intensity comes from metallic content that might cause a gastric reaction if a highly acid food (such as tomatoes) were eaten from it. Question: Would you ever consider eating tomatoes from *Indian Scout*?

Photorealism is one of the easiest of all schools of art to identify. This portrait of President Reagan and Vice President Bush, painted by Mike Hagel for Lynell, is titled *A New Beginning*.

All of us feel comfortable with cartoon art because we grew up with it in our comic books and daily newspapers. Cartoons such as Betty Boop, presented here in plate form by Lynell, make us smile.

One of the few examples of photography rather than an artist's rendering as art for a collector's plate is this example from a series featuring antique dolls issued by Seeley's Ceramics.

Prime time television shows and hit movies are big hits with collectors when transformed into the permanent art-on-porcelain of collectors plates. *Little House on the Prairie* was a plate series from paintings by Mike Hagel for Lynell.

Highly popular with a loyal (if specialized) group of plate collectors was the *Star Trek* series issued by the Hamilton Collection. The collector of this "pop" culture plate may or may not be a "Trekkie" and probably isn't a typical plate collector.

Collector's plate or souvenir plate? The dividing line gets thinner
with this 7¾-inch $19.95 plate, "The Young and the Restless."
Does the motif have any significance for those who haven't been
watching this soap opera?

In the 1970s a Canadian producer issued plates featuring classic steam locomotives. The plates sold well, proving not only that masculine-themed plates generate their own marketplace but that plates can be desirable wall decor. Here are 1994 issues, priced at $29.50 each.

Traditional themes are back in force. These two, "Golden Moments" and "Golden Retriever," have similar subjects and similar titles.

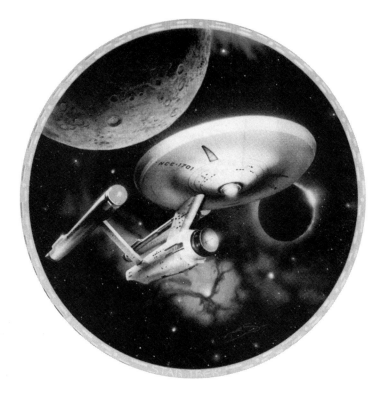

Typical of the attempt to capitalize on a trend is "USS *Enterprise*," an 8¼-inch plate with an issue price of $35. According to the producer, this is one of a number of plates in "The Voyagers" Plate Collection.

If more and more collectors are ignoring this type of writing and not responding to meaningless words such as "quality" and "service," it must be because the universe of collectors is finite. Those most likely to buy are those who see the most ads and mailing pieces, and when all these ads and mailing pieces begin to look alike the reader is numbed, not stimulated.

Even the magic two words "First Edition" have lost some of their punch because first editions no longer are rare, unusual, or even a novelty. In fact, some producers will stop dead in their tracks in the middle of a series and announce the next plate as the first edition of a new series, just to qualify for the implicit benefits of the two words.

Pitfall No. 5:
The Olympian Threat

Have you ever read an ad or mailer with copy such as this?

We expect demand to be enormous, and our allotment might well be sold out in a matter of weeks. I'd hate for you to be disappointed and have to buy this plate from another collector at whatever price that collector might determine, when you can have it now at original issue price..."

Hurled from Mount Olympus, this threat of being left out of mainstream action—or, worse, profit—

is a powerful selling argument. What's wrong with it is that usually it isn't true, as you learn when a year later you get that same mailing piece again or see the plate being discounted.

Another example of the Olympian Threat:

> If you had taken my advice in 1977 and bought the official Hallowe'en plate at the original issue price of $29.50, you'd be $150 ahead right now. If you'd bought *Jack Horner's Thumb* at $22.50, you'd have a plate now worth $100 . . .

Pitfall No. 6:
The Nonsense Claim

The Nonsense Claim invariably stems from a deadline. The magazine or newspaper demands that the advertiser deliver copy *now*, or the ad won't run. Panic! The ad isn't ready. So the advertiser creates headlines such as:

"You'll Be Glad You Called Us!"

"All the Best for Less!"

"For the Quality-Conscious!"

"More Than a Plate, But Why Take Our Word for It, See for Yourself"

"And Now for Some New Introductions . . ."

While we're wondering whether that last advertiser might have some *old* introductions, we see the implicit problem such advertising generates: Each claim is nonsense because each claim is chest-thumping without a single specific. How effectively does one thump his chest with a wet sponge?

Pitfall No. 7:
The Ignorant Declamation

The two of us shook hands on an agreement some years ago: We'd never patronize a business whose advertising or window signs formed a plural with an apostrophe before the letter "s." Even though we've sometimes gone thirsty when we wouldn't buy a Pepsi at a gas station with the hand-lettered sign, "Soft Drink's," we're firm in our stance. A roadside stand sold us no "Apple's" and a plate dealer sold us no "Limited Edition's."

Call it idiosyncrasy. We're convinced that others, given a choice, will do business with the more professional vendor; professionalism extends to the use of English.

Has the advertiser with the huge budget, selling a Chinese plate depicting a large bird and a panda, lost sales because he says his plate is "copywritten" instead of "copyrighted"? Maybe.

Has the mail-order company whose copy says that Pickard, founded in 1894, has been supplying fine china "for more than a century," lost sales because sharp-eyed collectors noted the discrepancy? Probably.

Declamatory ignorance breeds distrust and, finally, contempt.

An ad for a Christmas plate begins:

> "Think back to Christmas Eve, like when we were young, filled with the sounds and smells of Christmas magic..."

If we were filled with the sounds and smells of Christmas magic, we might be full but our house would be emptied of other people. And that word "like" parallels the useless verbalism, "You know."

Verisimilitude—The Appearance of Truth

If these pitfalls represent advertising a collector might not believe and to which a collector might not respond, what *is* the secret of effective communication to plate collectors?

The key lies in one word:

Verisimilitude.

Verisimilitude is the *appearance* of truth. We're all so heavily exposed to advertising messages we've grown cynical and skeptical, surprised when something we've bought turns out to be "as advertised." The rule of verisimilitude doesn't require a statement in an ad or mailer to be true; it simply should *appear to be* true.

We see an ad—the Bing & Grøndahl/Royal Copenhagen *Christmas Remembered* 1988 Christmas plate, issue price $65, for sale at $49.50. There isn't a word of descriptive copy in the ad. We go into the store or mail an envelope with a check for $49.50, and we get the plate. That's all there is to it: We believe the advertiser, and the next time he runs an ad we're his family.

For a company doing business by mail, the rule of verisimilitude means sending us a plate that actually looks like the picture in the brochure or the ad. For the producer, it means saying, "Available fall 1988," and actually making deliveries in the fall.

Thus we're always one step behind. Truth lags behind falsehood because some falsehoods are apparent immediately while truth becomes apparent only when the result is matched up to the original claim (at which time other falsehoods can become apparent too).

What to Believe and What to Ignore

How does the plate buyer know in advance which advertising to believe and which to ignore?

Our opinion is to ignore without further examination advertising which insults your intelligence—advertising which suggests that every first edition will give you marketplace performance parallel to the 1965 Lalique or 1971 Goebel Hummel.

Ignore advertising which is pompous, illiterate, or uninformed.

Ignore advertising whose adjectives ("The sinuous, lithe alertness of the jungle cat, every sleek motion a symbol of power and grace as he stalks his prey") don't match the picture (a sluggish, paunchy, out-of-proportion, muddy image of an amateurishly-drawn hydrocephalic panther).

Most important and most logical of all—

Ignore advertising whose approach—*or whose product*—is at variance from your own sense of taste. Follow that philosophy and you can't miss.

Chapter 11

Inter-Collector
Communications: Clubs
and Conventions

Two couples meet at their home airport, on their way to a plate convention. "We're going to have a great time," they agree.

The same couples meet at the Chicago or Los Angeles airport on the way home from the convention. "We had a great time," one couple enthuses. "We didn't," mourns the other. "We were bored, we spent too much money, the artists snubbed us, and we didn't learn much."

Both couples attended the same show. The moral of this too-common story? There's a right way and a wrong way to attend a plate show, and whether you enjoy yourself and get something out of it depends on just one person—you.

Travel, Hotel, and Registration

In the pioneer days of the late 1970s, when the entire universe of plate collecting was crammed into the old Quality Inn and the Albert Pick hotels in South Bend, no question about it—if you didn't stay at either of those two hotels, you were "out of it." The action was there, and those who stayed at other hotels and motels felt like outsiders.

Today, that isn't true. The key hotels, such as the Marriott in South Bend, reserve their biggest blocks of rooms for exhibitors and dealers, who are likely to stay in town twice as long as the typical visitor. The "action" in the lobby is of interest to producers. For collectors, the convention hall is the place to be.

Depending on your budget, you may not want to stay in the big hotels anyway. Usually, they're the most expensive. There's much to be said for staying in a smaller hotel or motel and having extra money in your pocket for buying that extra-special plate.

Almost every plate show of any consequence has a central office you can call or write to reserve rooms. We firmly recommend you set up your room reservations in advance. Otherwise you run the risk of scouting through the town, wasting hours to find a room 20 miles away.

We also suggest you pre-register. You'll save the magic component—time. When you go to a plate convention, you want every moment to count.

Some conventions have two admission prices— one by the day and the other for the whole show. If there's any possibility of your being there for the whole show, that's the package you should buy.

The one move you never should make is to buy a one-day admission, use it, then change your mind and try to trade in that one-day admission against a whole-show admission. A benevolent ticket-taker might let you get away with it, but it isn't playing the game the right way: What if everyone did it?

What to Attend?

Invariably, a plate show has so many seminars and functions you have to make a choice. Which ones are "musts," which ones would you like to attend, and which ones are outside your particular field of interest?

Some convention-goers spend so much time in seminars they never do get the flavor of the convention floor itself. Is this a mistake? Not necessarily. Many collectors are thrilled by the opportunity to meet producers and artists and don't care about the bustle and competitive atmosphere within the convention hall. That's their option.

Some seminar speakers are well-prepared and others just stand there waiting for questions from collectors to stimulate the session. We prefer a structured session. If a celebrity or authority agrees to be a speaker, that person should have enough respect for those in attendance to prepare some remarks.

The telling question for choosing seminars is:

Will you gain insight you didn't have before? To us, attending a seminar just to gawk at an artist isn't the most economical use of time, unless that artist explains how he or she painted the scene on the plate you own.

Good Manners Come First

We treasure our memory of this comment an outraged collector made at South Bend one year, referring to her encounter with an artist:

"I stood in line for more than fifteen minutes to get to her. Then, after signing my plates, she said she wouldn't sign the boxes."

Good manners used to be standard among plate collectors, but as artists become more available, familiarity seems to breed contempt. We've seen collectors express annoyance because an artist wouldn't agree with alacrity to travel 2,000 miles at that artist's own expense to address a plate club of 20 members. We've seen the "How dare you!" look form on the face of a collector who has monopolized an artist's time for 15 minutes while those standing in line get progressively more restless and finally suggest the individual move along. We've seen gregarious collectors break in on an artist's conversation with someone else.

Worst of all, we've seen collectors intrude on artists' privacy by standing over them like avenging angels while the defenseless artists are trying to have lunch or dinner, then tying them up with a conversation that by its length and its monologue-aspect shows no understanding of what good manners are.

Our suggestion, relative to encounters with artists (and producers, for that matter), is to set a two-minute time limit on what might be called "organized encounters"—for example, circumstances in which the artist crouches at a table, ready for the onslaught of plate-bearing collectors.

At a restaurant or in a hotel lobby, after verifying that the person you've spotted is indeed the plate artist Leonardo da Vinci, the proper way to make your admiration known is to catch the artist's eye, then say, "Mr. da Vinci, I'm Mary Jones, and I'm a collector. I just want you to know I love your work." Then move on. The artist will love you, Mary Jones.

Social Functions

At the dinner or banquet capping the convention, you not only can socialize with artists and producers to your heart's content; you can sit at the same table with them, dance with them, and impart (to their inevitable consternation) your own ideas of what subjects should be on the plate.

The atmosphere is different at the banquet. The frenetic pace of the convention has changed to a low-key, backslapping, "Hey-I-haven't-seen-you-for-almost-a-year" camaraderie. You aren't dispossessing someone else by spending fifteen minutes in conversation; and if you're sitting at the same table, you're *expected* to make dinner conversation.

Most conventions have some special functions. A producer will have a luncheon for dealers, or a manufacturer of transfers will have an open house for producers, or a plate distributor will have a cocktail party ostensibly by invitation only.

Please, please, don't "crash" one of these events. They aren't secrets, but they *are* private, and when you depend on the host's good manners to overlook your own bad manners, you're forgetting what you yourself would think if an uninvited guest showed up for a social affair you were hosting.

One distributor, who used to have a regular get-together for dealers, told us, "Never again. Some of these people think they're entitled to bust in on any affair, whether they're invited or not. I invited the dealers with whom we do business. They represented about a third of the people present. The rest were people who just wanted free hors d'oeuvres and drinks."

True to his word, this distributor has cancelled his dealer get-together. Another has given up on his annual breakfast (an event we ourselves have enjoyed each year—by invitation) because of "so many outsiders coming in."

The most curious breach of good manners is one we hope hasn't occurred to you: Pretending to be a dealer, to get discounts and invitations.

Horrified by the idea? Good for you. That means you wouldn't do it.

Have a Good Time!

Need we emphasize that on days when you're planning to spend hours touring the convention exhibits you wear comfortable shoes? Those fashionable but tight dress shoes and those four-inch spike heels are perfect for the banquet—but they'll do you in after a couple of hours on them as you wander on hard convention center floors.

The key point to remember, as you plan to visit a convention, is that *you're there to have a good time.* If you can do that, without a breach of good manners, you're the perfect convention guest!

How to Write a Club Newsletter

Not everyone can take the time and spend the money to attend a plate convention. But everybody can belong to a plate club.

And how do you know what's going on in a plate club? You read the newsletter. . . that is, if it's readable.

Remember the "Seven Deadly Sins" you learned in school all those years ago? Having read a batch of plate club newsletters, we can see seven different deadly sins which can kill off readership—or worse, membership. Here's how to recognize and avoid those seven deadly sins of plate club newsletter writing:

The First Deadly Sin

What's wrong with this, the first paragraph of a plate club newsletter?

> The Northtown Collectors Club is comprised of a group of individuals interested in various collectibles. While the main focus seems to be collectible plates, many members have other areas of interest such as figurines, bells, other art, etc. This makes for interesting programs.

Right! It's a classic example of the first deadly sin—*dullness.*

We rate dullness right at the top because a plate club newsletter can commit one of the other sins and not wind up in the wastebasket. But a dull newsletter is, by any method of judgment, worse than no newsletter.

How do you avoid the first deadly sin?

Easy: Write specifics, not generalities. Bury non-communicative stories deep on page 3 or 4, where they won't destroy readership the way they do on page 1.

The Second Deadly Sin

The second deadly sin is the simplest to control: *Hard-to-read format.*

The hardest-to-read we know of is typewritten copy, double-spaced, running the entire width of the sheet.

If you don't have the luxury of typesetting (and few do), use elite, not pica. Single space. Double space between paragraphs. Don't run the copy all the way across the sheet, but split the page into two columns (three if it's typeset). Use ruled lines to separate the elements. Bingo!

DON'T use one of those dot-matrix printers. They're okay for a financial report but hard to read and impersonal for newsletter use. A laser printer? Wonderful, if you have access to one. But don't go crazy with tricky little production gimmicks.

The Third Deadly Sin

What's wrong with this story?

Recently several members of the Club visited the charming home of a lady who has a complete collection of Hummel plates, etc. The afternoon was enjoyable.

Right! The only name in this story is Hummel, and she won't be reading the newsletter.

The third deadly sin is *lack of specifics.*

How much more readable the item becomes if the writer inserts a few names:

Saturday, March 9, four Club members—Mary Jones, Nancy Smith, Barbara Brown, and Lorraine Green— were invited to the Herman Johnson home. Wendy Johnson not only showed them her complete Hummel plate collection, including the valuable 1971 issue; she also treated the group to tea and biscuits and accepted a membership in our club.

What's the difference? Specifics. Mentioning names not only humanizes the story; it cements the club relationship with anyone whose name appears. Here's a rule you can apply with confidence:

> The more club member names you mention, the more intensively your members will read the newsletter.

The Fourth Deadly Sin

What's wrong with this paragraph?

> Norman Rockwell Night, postponed from its previous date, was combined with the Hibel presentation by Martha Kelly with films & slides including those shot at Palm Beach during the Club trip south.

Right! You have to read it three or four times to make sense out of it; and then you aren't sure you understand it.

The fourth deadly sin is *confusion*. You can avoid this sin by asking, after writing an article, "Would my mother understand it if I spoke it once?"

Separating components into logical segments ends confusion:

> We finally had Norman Rockwell night, which we had postponed from January 16. We combined it with a special Hibel presentation, at the February meeting. Martha

Kelly showed some of the films and slides she shot when she and other Club members visited the Hibel Museum at Palm Beach, Florida, last October.

The Fifth Deadly Sin

We won't write an example of this sin because you'll recognize it as soon as we describe it:

The fifth deadly sin is *egomania*.

You've read newsletters in which the same names—the club president, or the program chairman, or the editor of the newsletter, appear again and again. To the typical member, this suggests a two-level membership—an "elite" group to which the individual doesn't belong, and "those people" down below. What execrable public relations!

You can control the fifth deadly sin by establishing a helpful mechanical rule: No individual's name will appear more than twice in any issue.

The Sixth Deadly Sin

What's wrong with this paragraph?

Our Club commences its third annum with the April convergence. Among the intended endeavors will be a Swap 'n' Sell, an analytical dissertation on the art of Mary Cassatt by associate Helen Highwater, and savory refreshments.

Right! The writer is showing off. The sixth deadly sin is *phony intellectualism.*

If you're the editor of a club newsletter, or if you write articles for your newsletter, beware! The place to show off your massive vocabulary is the daily crossword-puzzle, not newsletter writing that supposedly communicates.

Hifalutin writing is two centuries out of date. Try reading a book written 200 years ago. It's tough slogging, and not just because of its outdated factual core. Today we have better ways to demonstrate our scholarship.

Write the way people talk and your story becomes readable:

> The April meeting begins our club's third year. Among the many exciting activities planned for this special meeting is a members only Swap 'n' Sell. Helen Highwater, our own Mary Cassatt expert, will give a short talk on that famous turn-of-the-century artist's techniques.
>
> To wind up the evening, we'll enjoy coffee, tea, and cakes. So bring your appetite for food as well as your appetite for information!

The Seventh Deadly Sin

Yes, the first sin, dullness, is the deadliest. But the seventh deadly sin is the killer, and it not only can murder a newsletter's readability; it can kill the club itself.

The seventh deadly sin is *apathy.*

Here's what happens: Someone says, "Let's have a monthly newsletter." Everyone is enthusiastic, and one member becomes editor. The first month is fun. The second month is less fun. The third month is a job. The fourth month is a chore. The fifth and sixth issues are combined. The decline has begun.

For a newsletter to flourish and prosper, not only does the club membership have to pitch in with articles and news; the editor has to have considerable dedication in two directions—first, to make the newsletter a public relations weapon of which the club can be proud, and second, to avoid the other six deadly sins. With that dedication, the seventh deadly sin won't exist.

Got it? Go and sin no more!

Chapter 12

Planning for the Future

Great-Grandma handed down to Grandma her most beloved personal treasure—her "good" set of dishes.

Grandma may, in turn, have handed them down to Mother, and we ourselves might still have incomplete sets of Spode, Castleton, or Haviland. We display the best pieces and occasionally look through ads placed by companies specializing in discontinued patterns, to see what it would cost to make our venerable set of dishes whole again.

"...In the Family for Generations"

Handing down fine china has been, in fact, a way of giving continuity to a family. We look at a piece in a china cabinet, and our hostess invariably says, "That's been in the family for generations."

To us as plate collectors, the message is clear: Plates can be a major part of the estate—if not financially, then certainly emotionally.

We say "...if not financially" despite memories of ads headed, "Woman Finds $1500 Dish In Attic." On the emotional/intellectual scale, plates weigh far more heavily on the emotional ("I love it") side than on the intellectual ("I'll make money from it") side.

Who Gets What, and How?

If you have more than one heir, consider: Even though your plate collection might not be a major component of your estate, shouldn't *you* be the one to determine who gets what?

Lists of plates have begun to show up in formally drawn wills; before you chuckle at the notion, put yourself in the position of two heirs, with unequal degrees of courtesy, deciding between themselves who gets *The Toymaker.*

You needn't formalize a bequest the way you might for a building or an automobile. But you'll be doing family and friends a favor if you make up a list of plates and, after each title, write the name of the person you want to own it if something happens to you.

(It's also a good way to start a plate inventory if you haven't made one up.)

Give the Accoutrements First

Whether as a donation, a bequest, or a gift, you can double the excitement and pleasure by splitting the gift in two.

Announce your gift by sending the Certificate of Authenticity (if one comes with the plate) and any enclosures. This becomes a gift in itself and builds anticipation for the plate.

Then, when you send the plate, it's as though you've sent a second gift. It's especially helpful if the person to whom you're giving the plate isn't a collector; getting the Certificate and accoutrements first is an introduction which makes the plate, when it comes, an old friend and not a stranger.

Post-Mortal Benefaction

If you have a "serious" collection—say, 100 plates or more—then you do have reason to formalize your post-mortal plans for them.

The Internal Revenue Service has attacked gifts and bequests far less valuable than a plate collection. Can you envision an agent, armed with a recent Bradex listing of plate evaluations, nailing your beneficiary with an inheritance tax? It can happen.

It *can't* happen if you make a "living gift" of parts of your collection. Suppose you have a son, daughter, or friend who has admired your *Lafayette*

Legacy series. Make the bequest now, with the provision that the plates stay with you while you're alive.

What you have, then, is a group of plates which another individual actually owns; but they're yours to enjoy while you live. That way, they aren't part of your estate, and they aren't taxable.

If you have a huge collection, start giving a few plates each year to those you want to own them after you're gone. This prevents the possibility of a huge, highly visible pile of valuable plates catching the taxman's attention.

WARNING AND DISCLAIMER! State laws and interpretations differ. Our suggestions aren't legal advice. Before making any move which might generate either estate or tax consequences, ask your own accountant or lawyer.

Donation Information

Another possibility exists, one ignored by collectors who wait for a local dealer to offer them the Bradex-listed value of each plate.

These individuals finally pay for newspaper ads, or run garage sales, or start piling undisplayed plates under the bed. The ads may cost them more than they take in, the people who come to the garage sale may drive cars over the lawn and steal tools from the garage, and the plates under the bed gather dust.

Here's another alternative:

Donate some plates.

The biggest benefit of donating plates is that the value becomes the *listed* value. Let's suppose you donate your *Lafayette Legacy* plates to a school. You can deduct, as a charitable donation, the listed value of the plates, as of the date you gave them.

If you have an incomplete series, or single plates you no longer want to show, let another family enjoy them: Donate them to the Salvation Army or a local thrift shop. Most organizations of this type are far more enthusiastic about getting collector's plates than they would be if you gave them worn-out clothing. And the word we get is that plates are much sought-after by bargain-hunters who frequent thrift shops.

Everybody benefits. You benefit in two ways: 1) You thin out your collection, making room for new issues, and 2) you get a tax-deduction for the listed value of the plates.

The organization benefits by acquiring fast-moving merchandise.

The ultimate buyer benefits by being able (probably) to own limited edition plates at below-listed price.

Plate producers benefit because once your collection drops below saturation level you're more inclined to buy more plates yourself.

Plate donations make sense not only as gifts to fund-raising organizations but also as gifts to religious institutions which have occasional sales and auctions; public television stations which have on-the-air sales and auctions; and non-profit groups to which you might belong.

A Few Sensible Rules

Let's superimpose two rules on any means of giving, bequeathing, or bestowing plates to other individuals or organizations:

1. Don't cheat and don't get greedy. This means not inflating the value of plates for tax-deductions. It means not claiming plates you didn't actually give. It means living with your conscience.

2. If your collection has genuine worth, consult a professional before making a firm move. This means phoning your accountant or your lawyer, explaining what you want to do, and asking for an official blessing. Unless you're an authority on the new tax laws (and no one seems to be, as yet), winging it alone can cause trouble you didn't expect.

(Example: When you claim a charitable deduction of more than $5,000, you need a written expert appraisal.)

But do weigh the value, emotionally as well as financially, of planned turnover of at least part of your collection. This is especially true of plates you don't display and have no intention of displaying.

Plate collections, like their owners, are "live" and ever-changing. Thinking of the next generation of owners can be a breath of fresh air for your collection—and for your own thinking.

Priming the Next Generation

Just who will that next generation of owners be? The typical plate collector doesn't watch "Sesame Street," doesn't go to rock concerts, and doesn't quite know who Molly Ringwald is.

As a couple of old fogies, we're unaffected by Pepsi-Cola paying $10 million to Michael Jackson as insurance for their "position" with the younger generation. We *are* affected by platemakers who ignore the demographics of their own business and don't care about wooing the next generation.

Suppose we were trying to interest children in classical music instead of plate collecting. We wouldn't confront them with Shostakovich's Fifth Symphony, for starters. Rather, we'd begin with Johann Strauss...Mozart...semi-classical Gershwin ...and end the concert with a rousing Sousa march.

The result? The kids might want to come back for the next concert.

With plates, it's equally unfair to stifle an embryonic interest by assuming they're as sophisticated in art and theme as we are.

For those who do care about instilling a love for plates in their children and grandchildren, we've developed a four-step formula for cultivating the latent tastes. No one is too young to be a plate collector!

The Four Levels of Appeal

We call the first level of collecting the "Clown and Cartoon" level. The second level is the "Animal and Doll" level. The third level is the "Current Hero" level. The fourth level is the "Beginner Appreciation" level.

We'll describe each level and give you examples. One preliminary point: Many adults, who think only "I want to buy what he or she likes" when buying a gift for an adult, change their attitude to "I want to buy what's good for the child's intellectual growth" when buying for youngsters. The result—when that gift is a plate—is something *we* like and the child doesn't understand. Lack of understanding = lack of appreciation.

So if you're starting off one of the kids on the pleasant lifelong road of plate collecting, don't immediately throw land mines in the road. Pave it with understanding: "I want to buy what the child will love."

It's surprising how many plates that appeal strongly to tots appeal to us too!

The First Level

Level One, the "Clown and Cartoon" level, is loaded with choices.

The Grand Old Man of clown paintings, Red Skelton, has given us a timeless legacy. Skelton, Ron

Lee, and any number of plate artists who know the universal popularity of clowns have given us a treasury ample enough to give a newborn a clown plate every year until age 100—and have plenty left over.

In this same category are the Schmid Peanuts plates—but hold it! These are dated, with *Mother's Day 1979* and *Christmas 1982* on them. If you give a dated plate, give it with an explanation.

Snoopy, Charlie Brown, and the Walt Disney characters are wonderful "starter" plates because a child doesn't regard the motif as threatening. That's also true of Raggedy Ann, also by Schmid, and Armstrong's *Woody Woodpecker* plates.

The Second Level

Level Two, the "Animal and Doll" level, has a wider range of potentials than any of the other levels.

We have horses (Fred Stone, American Artists) and bears (Tim Hildebrandt), kittens (Robert Anderson) and cats (Thaddeus Krumeich).

We have the classic Seeley dolls and the Jan Hagara dolls.

We have children with baby animals (Penni Anne Cross) and children with dolls (John McClelland).

We have a host of charming children in charming situations (Donald Zolan et al).

Any of these motifs of Level Two should be

understood—and so, welcomed and displayed with pride—by their juvenile recipient.

The Third Level

Level Three, the "Current Hero" level, is the next logical move up from the second level of collecting.

By the time a child begins to read, television and other entertainment media have given him or her a set of heroes. The heroes may be from a movie (*Star Trek* or *The Wizard of Oz*)...from sports (Steve Garvey or Reggie Jackson)...from the world of fantasy (*Alice in Wonderland*)...or from fairy tales (*Cinderella, Tom Thumb, Red Riding Hood, Sleeping Beauty*).

The adventurous will respond to Perillo's Indian plates, depictions of the Old West, and plates of Numa's now hard-to-get *Man's Dream of Flight*.

The slightly more sophisticated child may lean toward the professions for heroes. *The Age of Steam* series, showing classic locomotives, is wonderful wall decor for the engineer-to-be. On a considerably higher plane are plates such as *Future Physician* from the *Leaders of Tomorrow* series.

The Fourth Level

Level Four, the "Beginner Appreciation" level, is titled this way for the kids. But make no mistake, please: These are plates designed for adults, not their offspring or grand-offspring.

The reason we categorize them this way is that these are the plates which can be enjoyed on two levels. Adults love their simplicity, their lack of guile, their brightness. Youngsters like their understandable style, their uncomplicated art structure, their sense of innocence.

Example? Any plate by Ted DeGrazia. DeGrazia is the archetype of an artist whose work qualifies for this Fourth Level appreciation.

In this same category are many Norman Rockwell plates. The same characteristics that made Rockwell the most logical plate artist of all time make *some* of his art wonderful Fourth Level material.

But careful! When Rockwell became wry, his art was far too subtle for an under-12 collector. There are the heart-warming Rockwells; the patriotic Rockwells; and the humorous-situation Rockwells. Only the first group—plates like the early Gorham *Four Seasons* or the "Scotty" motifs—qualify as "safe" gifts to children. ("Safe" means the child will be the one who wants to hang it on the wall...and look at it.)

Quo Vadis

If we're going to have a next generation of plate collectors, let's start now. You and we have seen parents dragging bewildered infants through plate shows, occasionally pinning a free button on the child's blouse.

What does the young potential collector think? If that button shows Mr. Spock, we're safe. If it's an attitudinal reflection of Dr. Spock, we're still safe. But to the parents who think because they like a plate, their children will like it, we suggest: Pretend it's a book.

Chapter 13

Dealing with Dealers

"We don't get no respect."

Who said that? *Not* the typical plate collector.

Let's take a look at the relationship between the collector and the dealer/producer group. Sometimes, in order to get satisfaction, the collector has to involve everyone in the argument. Sometimes the collector is wrong, sometimes the dealer is wrong, and sometimes nobody and everybody is at fault in varying degrees.

As a collector, if you get a plate (especially one you've back-ordered) and think it isn't as advertised, when should you say and do what, and to whom? Let's explore the logical possibilities.

How Long Is "Approval" Time?

First, how about the length of time you can keep a plate before marching back to the store or packing it up in a mailing box to return it for a refund? In our opinion, plate dealers are extraordinarily benevolent on this point, especially with regular customers.

Compared with the business tactics of most other retailers and manufacturers, the attitudes and practices of business people in the plate universe are admirable.

We say this because we've seen dealers exposed to complaints that would cause Job to lose his temper: A collector brings in a plate, six months after buying it. The collector wants a refund. Why? "I decided I don't like it."

Try this tactic with any department store. Someone in the adjustment department, chosen for the job because of a cast-iron stomach, will explain patiently but firmly that satisfaction isn't guaranteed until the end of time.

It's an Individual Matter

Don't misunderstand us. Plate dealers are gentle folk, operating ladylike and gentlemanly businesses. But benevolence isn't universal. Lots of plate dealers don't offer an open-ended guarantee of satisfaction.

If you're the type who always second-guesses your original decision, get a clear understanding at the moment you buy the plate: Just how long can you keep it before the store owner can breathe a sigh of relief and enter your purchase on the books as "sold"?

Some companies who do business by mail make a big point of it: You have a whole year to decide.

Oh, don't worry about the seller standing behind this representation. Any mail order company knows: When the company puts a pledge in writing, then mails it, that company locks itself into the promise. If, after the transaction, the company hedges or tries to back away, the Federal Trade Commission and the U.S. Postal Service will come swooping in like hawks. They say it. They mean it.

But ask yourself, even as you buy the plate, whether you're buying it *because* you can return it. If you are, don't buy it. You won't give that plate a happy home.

As a general rule, tell the dealer you want to live with the plate for two weeks. That's long enough. Great heavens, if you bought clothing or a car, how long could you expect a 100 percent guarantee to last? But be sure the terms are written on the sales slip.

When dealing by mail, keep the sales literature on file. Invariably, the length of "examination time" is specified—15 days, 30 days, 90 days, one year.

A plea: Don't act like a "sharpie," holding a plate just to see if the value goes up, then sending it back. That isn't the spirit of plate collecting, nor of collecting any type of fine art.

If Your Plate Is Defective

Our advice, if your plate is defective, can be stated flatly in three little words: *Send it back.*

(See chapter 6, "When Is a Plate Defective—and What Can You Do About It?")

No matter where you bought it, no matter what the circumstances, no matter whether the plate was discounted or the dealer got only a handful and chose you to be one of the lucky few—send it back.

If the dealer looks at the plate and says, "That isn't a defect," be sure you're right. Don't invent a defect just to be able to return the plate. (This shouldn't be a problem anyway, since you surely would spot a defect within the initial inspection period.)

What's a defect? A crooked transfer. A warped plate. An out-of-line backstamp. A crack or chip (be sure *you* didn't put it there). "Dead" colors, compared to other plates of the same issue. Pits or pinholes in the plate surface.

No, *you* can't warp the plate. Nor can you screw up the backstamp or bleach out the colors. These definitely are defects. Your first job is to spot them as soon as you get your plate. Your second job is to get that plate off the market, because a manufacturer with integrity will tell a dealer: Smash a defective plate, send me the fragment of backstamp with my name on it, and I'll issue a credit or replace the plate.

Now, what if the dealer doesn't have another plate to give you to replace the defective one?

Our opinion: It's his responsibility to get you one. First of all, he should have inspected that plate before selling it to you. Second, he's the one dealing with the manufacturer, not you. So he gets on the phone with the producer.

(Obviously this rule doesn't apply to "back issues," plates in the secondary market. The producer is long since out of the ballgame.)

"He Kept My Deposit!"

Because we write a column for a plate collector publication, occasionally we hear from collectors who are justifiably outraged because a dealer took a deposit and never delivered the plate.

One such letter:

> I order quite a few plates each year. Most of the time, I have no complaints, but I have had two bad experiences with paying deposits on plates not in stock yet. The dealers both went out of business and kept my deposits—no refund or plates.
>
> One place had been in business for several years and sold out to someone else. The new owner told me the plates were not in stock but I informed him they had been on the secondary market for some time.
>
> Both of these places had been regular advertisers in a weekly trade magazine.

Here we have a sad circumstance, one which tarnishes the image of all plate dealers. For the collector who wrote this letter, chasing a shadow will be a waste of time and money.

Our advice: If you make a deposit on a plate not yet in stock, use a credit card. The dealer should write on the receipt, "This is a deposit on merchandise not yet delivered. If item is unavailable by [DATE], deposit will be returned."

Your receipt is no assurance of integrity, but you'll have a pretty good chance of getting a refund from the credit card company even if the dealer goes out of business.

When to Drag in the Manufacturer

Another letter to us says:

"For Christmas I received a plate called [NAME]. It came with a certificate, but not the right one. Whom should I write to, or what can I do about this?"

Again, your dealer should be your first stop. If the plate came from a recognized producer, the producer will have a file of unnumbered certificates, and the dealer should tell him to send you one, direct.

But dealers are people, and sometimes they forget to contact the producer, especially since writing for a replacement certificate is a no-profit contact (what a short-sighted attitude!). In that case, *you* write the producer. Feel free to tell the producer you've asked and asked and the dealer hasn't come up with the certificate.

When the dealer doesn't perform in a business-like manner, don't hesitate to express outrage. But reserve calls and letters to producers for cosmic issues. Other than giving up on a dealer who won't get you what you've paid for, we can think of three such circumstances:

1. A dealer repeatedly holds plates back, imposes a surcharge for popular new issues, or refuses to honor a commitment.

2. The producer announces an issue, then fails to

deliver it to the dealers or (if by mail) to the collectors.

3. The producer changes the plate blank, omits the promised certificate, delivers a plate with off-register or off-hue colors, or continues making plates after the pre-announced edition limit has been reached.

There's Power In Numbers

A suggestion: If you're contacting a producer, try to make that contact a *bulk* contact by a group, not just yourself.

A producer isn't particularly worried when an individual collector complains. When the entire membership of an 80-member plate club complains, adding the promise that the club will write all the collector publications unless an answer comes promptly, the producer is less likely to ignore the complaint.

So when a dealer says to you, "I can't get your plate for you. That's the way this producer is," first be sure the dealer isn't on the producer's "deadbeat list" for non-shipment; then load up your heavy artillery—your local plate club, or as many fellow collectors as will sign your letter—and fire.

Or, when you learn that dealer after dealer is hamstrung because collectors are clamoring for plates on which they've made a deposit, plates the producer promised to ship months ago, load up your heavy artillery and fire.

Neither a Patsy Nor a Bellyacher Be!

Plates are a personal business. In almost no other industry do customers know not only their dealer but the manufacturers behind their dealer.

We can add to that yet another dimension: Most plate artists have a high profile, and many collectors have met their favorite artists.

In the pleasant world of plates, where so many people know one another, no collector wants to be known as a chronic complainer. But neither does a collector want to be known as a doormat.

Between those two poles is a happy meadow where producer, dealer, and collector meet and discuss problems without the heat of heavy argument.

Turning that meadow into a battlefield is an unpleasant prospect. The decision to aim and fire should be made only when you the collector feel you've been exploited beyond any logical endurance. As the saying goes, "Don't fire until you see the whites of their eyes ...or their porcelain."

Chapter 14

Record-Keeping
Made Simple

Hey, when did we get that Bing & Grøndahl plate? And what did we pay for that unlisted plate with the cute kids on it? No, you're wrong. That's the Hummel you're thinking of.

Come on, help me remember. How can *I* figure what our collection is worth if *you* can't remember?

One of the joys of plate collecting is the permanence of your acquisition. That's why plates are such wonderful gifts: A box of candy may last a few days; a scarf may keep the giver's name fresh for several seasons. But a plate—you can visualize someone yet unborn asking, "Where did Grandma and Grandpa get this plate?"

That's only one reason for keeping respectable records of your collection. History can be fascinating.

Another reason is the somber possibility that someone will swipe some of your plates; record-keeping is one of the keys to protecting your plates. It adds *specificity* to an insurance claim, which means the insurance company is much less likely to become balky. (The next chapter discusses insurance.)

There's a third reason, a much brighter one: Keeping a record of your collection is fun!

What You Should Record

Here's the simple form we suggest for plate record-keeping:

On a sheet of paper, along the left margin, type these categories—

> Maker:
>
> Name of plate:
>
> Artist:
>
> Year of issue:
>
> Issue price:
>
> IF I BOUGHT IT—
>
> My price:
>
> Where I bought it:
>
> > Address:
> >
> > Phone:
> >
> > Individual's name:
>
> Date I bought it:
>
> IF A GIFT—

Who gave it to me:

Date:

Remarks:

Description of plate:

How limited:

Registration number if any:

Where I keep it:

Disposition if any:

Comments:

We think this approach is uncomplicated, complete, and useful in the future. It's personal, too, which is what this kind of record-keeping should be. You aren't preparing a report for the Internal Revenue Service.

A few points warrant explanation. You don't have to fill in every space. Most of the Danish Blue plates don't list the artist. Various plate reference books can give you the artists' names for back issues, but for heaven's sake don't look at these entries as an academic examination; it's your own record, for your own *enjoyment*.

For that same reason, we recommend allowing lots of space for "Remarks" about the circumstances of a gift-plate, and "Comments," for an ongoing chronicle. An example of comments, as you might compile a chronicle over a period of time:

Displayed in étagère.

July 1986—took to South Bend. Artist autographed it!

Christmas 1987—put in Aunt Jane's bedroom during her visit.

May 1988—stored in garage because new issue displayed in étagère.

One day in the future, next to "Disposition," an entry might look something like this:

December 1989—gave to Millie and Bob for their wedding.

You can see how a plate history can become, in microcosm, a family history. The more complete the record, the more valuable the history in years to come. Just one warning, though: Don't let record-keeping become a compulsive chore. You'll wind up hating it instead of loving it.

The Mechanics of Record-Keeping

We like a three-ring notebook, not only because it's roomy but also because the sheets can be shifted. This makes alphabetization a snap.

That, in fact, is why we suggest listing the maker first. This is the most logical way of alphabetizing, far simpler and less cumbersome than titles (which you might forget and which make you wonder whether to start with words such as "A," "An," and "The") or artist (who may be unknown or may be a partnership). We also suggest typing the category entries just once. Then head for the library or church or other location which has a copy machine, and run a bunch of copies. If you have—or plan to have—a collection of 50 plates or more, you might consider taking the original to an "instant printer" and letting him print copies. Usually an instant printer asks for a minimum of 100 sheets. Don't worry—you'll use them. And having a surplus means you won't worry about spoiling one.

You also might want to get a three-hole punch, so you can make your own notebook sheets and also so you can keep printed reviews or even ads adjacent to your own records.

Press clippings add spice to your collection. You won't find comments on every plate or artist, but it's astonishing how many articles you'll find. While you're at it, clip the occasional generalized stories about plate collecting that appear in the daily papers and consumer magazines. They can be a separate section in your notebook.

And oh, yes: Get a box of those little doughnut-shaped reinforcements, so your sheets won't pull loose out of the notebook cover.

If you're artistic, get a vinyl binder and create some original art on the cover; or clip out some reproductions of plates you own from magazines and transform the cover into an attractive montage of plate art. With press-on letters or your own careful calligraphy, give the book a title—"The [NAME OF FAMILY] Collector's Plate History," for example.

You'll have a volume you'll be proud to display for years to come—a true conversation piece.

An Extra Copy?

If you have access to a photocopy machine, no question about it: Make an extra copy of your plate record. Update that spare twice a year.

Why? If a friend wants to borrow one of your records, you won't have to let the original out of your possession. If for some reason you take a sheet out of the master book, you have a safe copy of that sheet.

Most significant, if something happens to your collection or part of it, you have a backup record.

That's the core of having a second copy. It won't be worth much if you keep it right next to the original. Wrap it in aluminum foil and put it where it's least likely to be affected by fire or flood. Or leave it with a neighbor.

All this presupposes you take plate collecting seriously. But of course you do: You're reading this book, aren't you?

Chapter 15

How to Be Sure
Your Plates Last
a Lifetime

Just as you're about to put your $85 collector's plate in the dishwasher, you pause. That lovely art won't come off in hot water, will it, leaving you with a blank plate?

Then, when you hear the 150-degree water hissing over the porcelain, you panic.

You yank the dishwasher open. In the clouds of steam, you find your beloved plate, and it's—

What's your guess? Does a dishwasher damage your plate?

The answer is no. A dishwasher won't damage the *picture* on your plate. But this is a qualified no, and if you've been washing your collector's plates that way you may unwittingly have been playing a game of Russian Roulette.

The odds shift heavily against you if you use dishwasher detergent, which can dull some colors and react chemically with others to fade them.

All Plates Are Not
Created Equal

Theoretically, hot water won't hurt your plate. After all, water turns to steam at 212 degrees Fahrenheit, and your plate became porcelain at close to 2,000 degrees hotter than that. The picture went on at about 1400 degrees, so what's the fuss?

We see two reasons for treating your plates more gently. First, does it have a gold band? Take a look at some of your dinnerware or drinking glasses that have gold bands. If you've had them in the dishwasher a dozen times, or even less, you'll find the gold wearing off at some spots. That's because the gold *isn't* fired on at 1400 degrees—it would turn to ash at that temperature. So the gold isn't as permanent as the rest of the plate.

Second, how do you know when your dishwasher will act up and shake that plate, perhaps onto a vibrating rack that despite porcelain's well-earned reputation for toughness could result in a crack or a chip?

Why Take The Chance?

Our own collector's plates never see the inside of our KitchenAid. We treat them the same way we treat our Waterford crystal and some of the expensive decorator pieces we've acquired over the years—with respect.

Don't use any detergent that has a bleaching agent in it. Don't use any scouring powder or abrasive. We prefer hand-washing (after all, you won't go through this more than once a year, if that) in warm, not hot water. The rule is, if your hands can't stand it, your plate can't stand it.

Don't use a towel which leaves lint and strings all over your plate. You'll forever be picking pieces of thread off the face of your plate.

If someone has dripped gunk all over your plate and you can't get the oily mess off without heavy rubbing, let it stand in the sink, in mild suds, for 10 to 20 minutes. The mess should wipe off.

European plates with hanging holes in the back can develop rust spots if you've strung wire through the holes. Resist the impulse to use Brillo: You'll get rid of the rust, but probably scratch the glaze. Instead, use one of the commercial rust removers.

Wood Metal, Stone, and Whatever

You'd think a metal plate would be tougher and less subject to damage than porcelain. Not true!

Metal plates are like children playing games—they accumulate scratches and abrasions without even trying.

We know some people who spray their metal plates, especially copper ones, with acrylic "finishing" spray. The spray won't damage the plate, but it adds a gloss you may not find attractive; and if you don't spray with great care, you'll find big drops where rivulets of spray have accumulated and hardened.

When you get a fingerprint on a metal plate, don't use a copper or brass cleaner if your plate has a lacquer coating—and most do.

The lacquer prevents tarnishing, but it can come off if you rub it with a cleaner. You then have to remove all the lacquer and either relacquer or resign yourself to repeated polishing.

Wood requires an entirely different chemistry. We ourselves don't have any wooden plates, but several collectors who do tell us they use ordinary furniture polish or lemon oil.

Don't be afraid to polish your silver plates with the same gentle silver polish you use for your other silver pieces.

With a stone or crushed glass plate, such as Incolay or Avondale, sometimes you literally have to steam-clean the surface to get rid of discolorations. It's parallel to cleaning a building.

Some "composition" plates (Incolay, Avondale, Cinnabar) have metal backstamps inset into them. A typical room in your home will alternate between summer moisture and winter dryness, and if that metal is affixed with glue, it can come loose.

We suggest checking these plates each season. If

the backstamp seems wobbly, take the plate off the wall, use a white glue to reset it, let the plate sit on a table for 24 hours, then rehang.

Storing and Moving

If you want to assure yourself of some broken plates, stack them flat in a shipping box when you're storing them or moving.

Standing them on edge will improve the possibility of unbroken plates. Have plenty of padding above, below, and especially on the sides. You may not have the commercial styrofoam chips (called "popcorn" in the trade), but you have newspapers. Don't just lay the newspapers into the box. Crumple them into tight balls which add resiliency to absorb impact.

Porcelain doesn't deteriorate in storage. If you think your collection will sit in the box for months or years, put each one into a plastic bag for additional protection.

The heat buildup in an attic or the dankness of a cellar won't have the slightest effect on your porcelain plates, unless you have a sudden, sharp change of temperature; but if the change were that drastic, the house would be gone too.

If you have an especially valuable plate, don't give it to the movers at all. Put a urethane foam pad on the floor of your car, and that's where your plate rides. It'll take up residence in your new location in the same flawless condition it was in when the ride started.

Don't put the plate on the seat—use the floor. A sudden stop could result in a porcelain shower if your plate is on the seat.

We've said it many times: Porcelain is *tough*. But a plate falling onto a metal seat-belt retainer, or onto another plate, can crack, especially if it's the result of braking which adds velocity to the drop. Why risk it?

The Annual Checkup

Once a year, check each plate to see "how it's doing." There's one, hanging on a nail; has the nail become rusty? Is the plaster loose around it? Don't worry it to death, but if you sense a lack of permanent "hold," take it down.

The worst thing you can do is jiggle the nail as hard as you can to tell whether or not it's still firmly imbedded. Sure enough, your jiggling will loosen a nail that otherwise would have stayed put for years.

If a plate is on a stand, check the hinges. Are they tight or loose?

Here's a plate hanging over an ebony piano. What would happen if that plate fell? You'd damage *two* treasures. Better find another place for it.

If You Break a Plate...

Yes, you'll find shops that do "invisible" repairs on porcelain. We never yet have seen one of those invisible repairs that was truly invisible.

If you collect plates as an investment and break one, forget it. Your plate never, never will be worth what you'll spend to repair it.

If, though, you collect only the plates you think look good, and you break one you can't replace, a repair may be in order. Depending on the deftness of the repair person (and of course the kind of break), you may wind up with a near-invisible repair job. Sometimes the motif on the face of the plate can be retouched, but this is a "band-aid," not a permanent repair. It shows up immediately under the black light inspection professionals give a valuable plate before buying it.

Our opinion is: If you can get another plate without spending half your annual income, do it. You'll never be satisfied with that repair, and your eye will go to it every time you look at the plate.

And in Conclusion, Ladies and Gentlemen...

There's no substitute for common sense in caring for your plates.

One of the best bits of advice we can offer is:

Treat your plates as you would your face

You wouldn't use sandpaper on your face. You wouldn't scrub it using a brush with wire bristles. You wouldn't pour acid on it.

Treat your plates the same way, and a hundred years from now, no matter what kind of shape *you're* in, your plates will be gorgeous. If they aren't, call us a hundred years from now to complain.

Chapter 16

Potpourri

Let's take a quick look at some of the points we may not have covered...such as current happenings and what the specific words mean.

Trends and Probabilities

Traditionalists are continually outraged.

That's as true of plate collecting as it is of politics, music, and business.

So it's normal for old-line collectors to ask, "What's going on here?" when they see a handsome porcelain plate on which appears the likeness of—

- Reggie Jackson, the baseball player...

- Don Mattingly, a not-as-well-known baseball player...

- Leonard Nimoy, the actor, portraying "Mr. Spock" in *Star Trek*...
- Norman Rockwell sketches, obviously too primitive to ever be intended for public viewing...
- Scenes from *The Red Badge of Courage*, a quickly-forgotten television mini-series...
- Elvis Presley...
- Richard Petty, the cigar-smoking race car driver...

In our opinion, what these plates have in common is their short life span. One short generation from now, who will know who Leonard Nimoy and Don Mattingly were? Who will want "celebrity" plates depicting celebrities who no longer have any entertainment value or sociological impact?

As we say, that's our opinion. Each of these concepts may not last long enough to qualify as trends. A better term: Fads.

The Rockwell Phenomenon

Norman Rockwell died in 1978. For the last few years of his life, his once prodigious output of art dwindled to near-zero.

Couple this with a problem:

Rockwell was and is far and away the most popular plate artist. But as we state elsewhere in these pages, some of his art was unsuitable for plate motifs; and even though he painted many hundreds of subjects, the universe of Rockwell paintings is finite.

Rockwell art is becoming an expensive commodity for producers. The Norman Rockwell Estate Licensing Company has supplanted Curtis Publishing Company (publisher of *The Saturday Evening Post*, for whom Rockwell painted hundreds of covers) as licensing agent, and Norman Rockwell's casual and paternalistic view toward use of his art has long since been replaced by advances against royalties.

So what to do?

Plate producers have seen two solutions: First, they have begun issuing Rockwell art which never should have been released onto plates. The Rockwell acceptance level of collectors being what it is, the very name "Rockwell" will mean considerable sales.

In our opinion, the slow decline has begun, and inferior Rockwells are feeding that decline. Some producers of Rockwell collectibles, who grew fat in the anything-goes period of 1976-1983, have passed from the scene. Others are reissuing illustrations they used before, because in 1988 the name Rockwell no longer means automatic profit.

The Filtration Process

Rockwell is indicative of collecting as a whole. Collectors are fussier and more knowledgeable than they were a decade ago. The marketplace is "tighter," and salesmanship is back in vogue.

It isn't as easy to issue your own plate as it was a decade ago, either. Then, you could inveigle a transfer house to "proof" a lithographic motif for less than $1,000. Today, $4,000 to $5,000 is the rule, and if they don't know you the transfer houses want cash in advance.

The dollar is down against the yen, and plate "blanks" from Japan cost about 40 percent more than they did in 1982 and 1983.

The result: Fewer producers are making plates . . . but those who can show a track record of having issued more than two or three plates are probably on solid financial ground.

What About Birds, Children, and Furry Animals?

If you're appalled by baseball players and race car drivers cluttering up your hobby, be of good cheer. There's no slackening in the output of birds, non-ferocious animals, and children.

Nor is there a slowdown in the technique of reaching back into history for artists. Turn-of-the-century art has been sifted through so often there's little left; but 16th through 19th century artists represent an unused storehouse of many thousands of paintings.

So Grandma Moses, Mary Cassatt, J.C. Leyendecker, and Bouguereau already have begun to be joined by the shades of Winslow Homer, Raphael, and Eduard Manet. Experiments with Pablo Picasso and Salvador Dali failed, but that was when the world of plate collecting was younger.

Plate Producers: The Passing Parade

Some who once were "big names" in plate production have passed from the scene or merged into other companies.

Veneto Flair and its "Studio Dante de Volteradici" are now part of the Bradford Empire. River Shore's plates are issued by other producers. The Ghent Collection, Hackett American, Kern Collectibles, Wildlife Art, and a dozen others have passed from the scene. The giants, Bing & Grøndahl and Royal Copenhagen, have combined their U.S. operations.

How does this affect the collector?

Unless you've prepaid for a plate that never will appear, it shouldn't affect you at all. To a collector, the *who* should be subordinated to the *what*. In plainer English: If you collect plates you like, plates whose art appeals to you, then the name of the producer is of no consequence. What matters is the art on the plate.

This concept is the great equalizer, the catalyst that holds producers and collectors together.

As long as producers remember they have collectors to please, we'll have an ongoing and exhilarating hobby, one in which we can count on happy surprises each time we visit a store or open a piece of mail catering to our pastime.

Chapter 17

Plates with a Future

The crystal ball is cloudy today—as it always is.

As long as you and we both realize this, here are some speculations about "plates with a future"—plates whose values may rise over the next few years.

1. *Women of the Century*

This twelve-plate series was issued by D'Arceau-Limoges, through the Bradford Exchange, between 1976 and 1979. It never was offered to conventional retail outlets, which may have stifled increases in the secondary market.

Recently, collector interest seems to have picked up. The first plate, *Scarlet en Crinoline*, was issued at $17.64 (the strange amount is due to the original price in French francs). For no apparent reason it recently increased in listed value from $24 to $30. That's only six dollars, but it also is 25 percent. Worth watching.

2. Royal Copenhagen/Bing & Gr∮ndahl, *American Mother's Day*

The first issue of this new series is the 1988 plate. Issue price is $34.50. Title is *Western Plains*. The small (5¹/₈″) Royal Copenhagen plate has the typical soft bas-relief with underglaze wash.

Unlike some Danish plates, which collectors can buy in Europe for considerably less than the U.S. price, distribution of this plate is aimed at North America, eliminating the "gray market" in Danish plates.

Another reason for collectibility is the closed-end series. Unlike most Danish series, which go on forever, the *American Mother's Day* series will end with the tenth plate.

3. *Age of Steam*

These are Canadian plates by Christian Bell Porcelain, and they never have been easy to get in the United States.

The art—steam locomotives—is superb, the colors intense, and the production near-perfect. When these plates first appeared in 1981 (first edition: *Symphony In Steam*, issue price $75, edition limit 15,000) some "experts" dismissed them as too masculine.

In more recent years, plates as wall decor have come into their own, and these handsome, ageless motifs are more sought-after now than they were even a few years ago.

4. *Russian Fairy Tales*

Some dealers still have these elegant Villeroy & Boch plates at or near their original $70 issue price. Our opinion: If you collect for both beauty and investment, you won't make a mistake by grabbing these.

This is especially true of the first edition, *The Snow Maiden*, if only because first editions traditionally bring more in the secondary market.

The theme may be somewhat obscure for American tastes, and this may be what kept these plates from being an instant winner. But the splendid art stands by itself, even unexplained—and this is one great criterion for judging the eye-value of a plate.

5. Studio Dante de Volteradici—any plates

Underground word is that production difficulties may end all manufacture of these high-relief sculptured plates. If that happens, we see a powerful reason for the value of any de Volteradici plates to increase in value:

These are the only plates using the medium of what the producer calls "Ivory Alabaster."

Obviously the plates aren't alabaster stone; they're compressed gypsum. But good looking they are, and over a couple of years their color changes to a slightly yellowish cast, just as real ivory piano keys do.

The original de Volteradici plates, the *Grand Opera* series, never seemed to show much value increase. Last time we looked, the first edition, *Rigoletto* (1976), issued at $35, listed for $37. One problem seemed to be the sudden discontinuance of the series in 1982, after the seventh plate—a peculiar series length.

You can't miss a de Volteradici plate. It looks like no other. That's why we think the curio value will be high if indeed production stops.

6. *Twinkle, Twinkle, Little Star*

John McClelland always has been a popular

plate artist, and in our opinion this 1987 issue from Reco is one of his best. It shows a little girl in a quiet flower-filled meadow, looking at the starry sky.

The producer—one of the most reputable in the world of plates—says this is the first edition of a new series, *Treasured Songs of Childhood*.

The first edition of McClelland's *Mother Goose* series, *Mary, Mary*, has gone through the roof. Issued at $22.50, it lists at presstime at $205 and has been higher. *Twinkle, Twinkle, Little Star*, issued at a time when competition is less than *Mary, Mary* faced, could be McClelland's next big winner.

7. U.S. Historical Society stained glass plates

The United States Historical Society first used a stained glass technique for its annual Christmas plate (edition limit 10,000). The $10^{1/4}''$ plate has a cathedral glass "round" with colors fired into it for permanence; the round is set into a pewter rim.

In recent years this producer has expanded the stained glass plate medium to include subjects such as Robert E. Lee, various ships, and historical subjects.

The reason for our enthusiasm about the stained glass plates is their magnificence when light streams through them. The plates rank among the most decorator worthy, and their price—averaging $135 to $160—positions them at the elite upper end of the collecting spectrum.

8. *Carrousel Prince, Carrousel Princess*

Issued by Anna-Perenna, these $75 plates exemplify the best of (Ms.) P. Buckley Moss's highly stylized art. The edition size is small—5,000—which should help maintain market value.

Carrousel horses traditionally are strong sellers, and these two plates are especially attractive because they combine charm with a recognized artist's distinctive style.

At presstime, the producer announced a third plate with a full carrousel motif. The ensemble is titled *Carrousel Triptych*, but whether the third plate—$9^3/4''$ as opposed to the $8''$ size of the first two—will complement the others or add confusion is too speculative a guess, even for us.

(One additional note: You, as we, may spell the word *carousel*. Either spelling is correct.)

9. *Treasures of the Doré Bible*

What makes these plates possible winners is the same factor underlying the de Volteradici plates: They're different.

A distaff artist named Merri Roderick and a little-known producer named Rhodes Studios have issued *Moses and the Ten Commandments*, the first plate in this series—in bronze relief.

We're uneasy about this prediction because the producer describes the plate as "fused bronze," a term we never heard before. If the plate is cold-cast bronze, artificial terminology suggests too strong a sense of showmanship.

Still, we like the idea of bronze plates, and we suspect many who regard porcelain as a mundane medium will be drawn to *Treasures of the Doré Bible*.

10. Your choice

This isn't a copout. Instead, it's a reminder: You can't make a mistake if you buy only plates you'd enjoy viewing every day for the next 20 years.

It confounds us when an otherwise sane individual buys a plate because he or she has an inside tip: "This plate will skyrocket in value." The plate is ugly, the art is coarse, the theme is a rock star or athlete or television show which won't be recognizable ten years from now.

Secure in its original box, the plate goes under the bed or into a corner of the closet, waiting for its star to rise.

Wrong reason! The wonder of plate collecting is the joy of owning art in such a displayable form. If the value goes up, be doubly glad. But if you've collected plates for a while, how many of the plates you really love have you even considered offering for sale, even at 50 percent more than you paid?

Neither would we.

Chapter 18

The Turbulent 1990s

As the last decade of the twentieth century took form, erosion hit the ranks of plate collecting.

Three bases underlay the deterioration of the plate market:

1. Saturation on the part of the original cadre of collectors, who had helped launch the phenomenon in the mid-1970s and had loyally collected plates until every corner of the household was covered.

2. Sameness of themes, leading even the most dogged collectors to ask, "How many Rockwells, how many Indian children, how many fuzzy animals are we supposed to swallow?"

3. Wild claims of value-appreciation, accompanied by heavy overproduction—an expression of producer-cynicism that eventually had to spread to the ranks of collectors themselves.

The "Plate Depression" lasted from 1989 until 1993. By mid-1993, the big producers had re-established a pre-depression schedule of plate issues.

Meanwhile, most had added dolls, figurines, cottages, and music boxes to their lines. Plates became one of many "products," no longer the bellwether of collectibles.

What Happened to the Dealers?

Suppose you're a dealer. You think you're still in the golden decade (1976-1986).

But you aren't.

You've become an adjunct, an ancillary, an extension of mainstream plate collecting. Except for the original plate producers—Bing & Grøndahl/Royal Copenhagen and Goebel—you account for 10 percent or less of total plate distribution.

Yet, you're at the mercy of collectors who acquired their plates elsewhere. They've decided to trade them in...or, worse for you, sell them.

During the Golden Decade, you'd buy those plates for whatever amount below their "listed" price and anticipate reselling them to another customer.

Uh-oh! What other customer? The next 10 customers are like the first one, selling plates instead of buying them. How long can you stay in business when you've switched roles—you've become the collector, paying for plates, and your customer has become the dealer, selling them?

So only the fittest—and the most dogged—have survived among the dealer ranks.

Our recommendation: Patronize those dealers. They deserve it!

Rock Around the Clock... At Least for Today

The hot sellers *to new collectors* during the interregnum have been plates showing Elvis Presley in one pose or another—his post-mortem licensing agents are heartless—and the Beatles.

So we have Elvis plates titled "Viva! Las Vegas" and "Heartbreak Hotel" and "Hound Dog" and "G.I. Blues" and "Concert in Wichita" and "USS *Arizona* Benefit" (average selling price at presstime about $30).

So we have Beatles plates titled "The Beatles '65" and "Help!, Shea Stadium" (average selling price at presstime about $28).

No question: Elvis and the Beatles have fan clubs whose longevity has transcended the performing life span. As symbols of one facet of their time, they're as plateworthy as Mickey Mouse, aren't they?

Is Garvey Marvy? Is Spock Schlock?

No, we haven't lapsed into gobbledygook; but during the mad but totally understandable panic to stay in business during the Plate Depression, some plate producers did—at least as far as old-time collectors were concerned.

One of the guiding philosophies of *all* art collecting is *timelessness*. Will what you've collected possess a universality your descendants, generations from now, can enjoy?

The Mona Lisa is timeless. Winged Victory is timeless. Art by Renoir and Van Gogh may not be timeless, but it certainly transcends a single century.

Now comes a collector's plate. What's the image on it? Baseball players Steve Garvey and Carl Yastrzemski. Basketball player "Magic" Johnson. Football players Joe Montana and Lawrence Taylor. And, apparently, any semi-name athlete who would sign a contract and autograph some plates.

Nolan Ryan, shortly after announcing retirement, had his baseball cards reissued as porcelain *cards*, 2½" × 3½". Because they're porcelain, some hyper-purists equate them with plates. They aren't.

Just what are these issues? Collectibles or novelties?

Our vote: They're novelties.

Our justification for our vote: We don't have to wait for centuries. Ten years from now, someone will look at that plate (assuming it's still displayed) and ask, "Steve Garvey? Who's he?"

And even a single generation from now these specialty plates will be as incomprehensible to the casual viewer as "23 Skidoo" and "Yes, We Have No Bananas."

Please, please don't regard this judgment as brutal. Plates are a broad enough medium to encompass novelties, timeless art, and the huge limbo in between. What has irritated the original cadre of collectors, and driven some of them from the ranks, is the *claim* that a novelty is a work of art.

Now comes Mr. Spock.

Mr. Spock?

Oh, Mr. Spock is just one of many plates from the television show "Star Trek." And "Star Trek" is just one of many television shows whose light flared brightly and temporarily on the 21-inch screen and was reflected with some permanence on an 8½-inch plate.

Most peculiar plate candidate: The cast of the television show "The Young and the Restless." On the air for 20 years, this soap opera (so advertised by its issuers) hardly qualifies as the subject of a plate with universal appeal.

What Happened to Norman Rockwell?

What happened to Norman Rockwell? Overproduction.

Certainly it was no secret in the 1980s that a Rockwell plate was sure-fire. Producers unearthed not only the old dependables, covers of *The Saturday Evening Post*; they tore the covers off ancient copies of *The Literary Digest*; they unearthed advertising for which Rockwell had painted the illustrations; they found sketches and early, non-representative work; they used up the paintings of Leyendecker, whose Rockwell look-alikes had preceded Rockwell himself at *The Saturday Evening*

Post; they hired artists adept in photorealistic technique to paint Rockwell-like scenes.

And, eventually, when the Rockwell plate market softened, they issued Rockwell figurines, Rockwell plaques, Rockwell mugs, Rockwell trays, Rockwell prints, and Rockwell images on almost any reproducible medium that exists.

No, they didn't kill Rockwell. His sense of the Americana that was still is the most superb depiction of those kinder, gentler times. But Rockwells have become so common the term "collectible" could barely apply.

Will Rockwell return? Unquestionably. The art is too plate-perfect to disappear. The only problem: Rockwell died in 1978. Every known piece of art has been gobbled up. Any "new" Rockwells won't be new at all. Look for different media (other than porcelain), different border treatment, unusual sizes and shapes, and blended images. All these stem from a single realization: There just ain't gonna be no new Rockwells.

The Old Favorites Are Back

A proud, spirited horse.
A mouse family at Christmastime.
A puppy with its mother.
A baby with its mother.
Winsome children, with or without mothers.
Peaceful woodland animals.
Birds on the wing.
Flowers.

Mythical creatures.

Since the beginning of organized plate collecting, these motifs have been "safe"—evergreens.

They're back, and they're back in force.

Some of the most collected plate artists, such as John McClelland, Sandra Kuck, Pat Buckley Moss, Edna Hibel, and Donald Zolan, never were out of fashion and survived the Plate Depression. As the new Golden Age dawned, these "Old Dependables" were acquiring a new generation of collector-admirers, without ever having lost their original coteries. That they had survived the dark days is a tribute to their ability—and that of those who issue their plates—to maintain a universal visual appeal, on the level of collectors old and new.

To understand the significance of this spurt in traditional themes, go back to the mechanics of platemaking. The single most expensive element in the issuance of a plate is the proofing and production of the transfer.

Even since the first edition of this book, transfers ("decals" to the trade) have moved into the electronic age. A century ago, all transfers were color-separated by hand. Then photographic color separations reached a point of near-perfection. Today, huge scanners with many "gigabytes" of computer memory can generate color separations in a flash. But the scanners are expensive, and the transfers they create are expensive.

So to issue a plate means ordering X-thousand transfers. During the Plate Depression, few plate producers wanted to take this risk. Many plates issued during the 1989-1993 period were reissues or used "stock" transfers.

So the resurgence of familiar themes, with fresh art, is a powerful symbol of the rebirth of plate collecting.

Is a new Golden Age of Plate Collecting dawning? Ask us five years from now, when the next edition of this book is in preparation!

Glossary

AGATEWARE

Ceramic veined and mottled to resemble agate.

ANNUAL

A plate issued once each year, with common theme.

AT ISSUE

The retail price of a plate at the time of issue.

BACKSTAMP

Text on the back of the plate, usually inside the footrim. Usually this text includes the plate title, artist's name or signature, maker's name, year of issue, position of plate within a series (if any), edition limit, and individual serial number.

BAS RELIEF

Dimension on a plate, such as the Incolay plates, in which the motif stands away from the background.

BISCUIT

A plate that has been fired but not glazed.

BLANK

Undecorated glazed ceramic body, whether plate, bowl, cup, or other shape, ready to be decorated and fired.

BONE ASH

Powdered animal bones, added to the china formula to give translucency and whiteness.

BRADEX

A listing of plate evaluations, limited to those plates listed by the Bradford Exchange.

CELADON

Translucent greenish glaze invented by the ancient Chinese, later used in Korea and Japan. A number of contemporary porcelain houses list a "celadon" color, but the original formula has been lost, and modern methods can't duplicate the original delicacy.

CERAMIC

Generic term applied to any item made from clay and hardened by firing (including all earthenware, stoneware, china, bone china, and porcelain).

CERTIFICATE OF AUTHENTICITY

A paper accompanying a plate, attesting to its position within a limited edition. If the plate is numbered, the identical number appears on the certificate.

CLOSED-END SERIES

A plate series with a pre-announced number of motifs. After the final motif, the series ends.

COBALT BLUE

The deep blue color resulting from firing cobalt oxide at high temperature. The Royal Copenhagen plates are colored by cobalt.

COUPE SHAPE

A plate concave from center to outer edge, with no shoulder (rim).

CREAMWARE

Soft-bodied china, cream color with a high gloss glaze finish, made primarily in the Ohio Valley of the U.S.

EARTHENWARE
Unvitrified china.

EDITION LIMIT
The maximum number of plates which will be produced of an individual plate issue.

FELDSPAR
One of a group of crystalline minerals consisting of aluminum silicates plus either potassium, sodium calcium, or barium, used to give additional hardness to china. Petuntse is a form of feldspar.

FIRST EDITION
The first motif in a plate series.

FOOT-RIM
The raised ring around the bottom of a plate.

GERMANWARE
Extremely hard stoneware *(Steinzeug)* made in the Rhineland, often glazed with a salt-mix, resulting in a slightly pitted surface.

GLAZE
The glassy finish applied to a plate. Typically, a plate is fired before the application of glaze ("biscuit" firing) and again after the application of glaze ("glaze" firing). Most motifs are fired onto the glaze, but some, especially the Royal Copenhagen plates, may have their motifs applied before the glaze firing.

JASPERWARE
Unglazed stoneware developed by Josiah Wedgwood, stained before firing in any color (although "Wedgwood Blue" is the predominant color). Jasperware is usually decorated with a low relief white design, simulating a cameo.

KAOLIN
Clay, the basis of porcelain.

MOTIF

Work of art which appears on the face of the plate.

OPEN-END SERIES

An ongoing series of plates with no announced termination.

OUT-OF-ROUND

Imperfect plate, lopsided or not perfectly circular.

PARIANWARE

Lustrous, translucent, creamy, thin china resembling parian marble (from which it takes its name). Example of Parianware: Irish Belleek.

PLATE PRICE TRENDS

A listing of plate evaluations which appeared in the now defunct *Plate Collector* magazine.

RELIEF

See "Bas relief."

SECONDARY MARKET

The trading or selling of plates after the producer has ended production.

STONEWARE

Fully vitrified ceramic, not as translucent nor as thin as most porcelain or china.

SWAP-'n'-SELL

An event at many plate conventions in which collectors bring their plates, displaying them for sale or trading.

TERMINAL DATE

A means of establishing an edition limit; the last day on which firing will be scheduled.

TRANSFER

Metallic pigments on paper. When wet, the pigments slide off the paper onto the plate, much as a decal slides off its paper base. Firing the plate fuses the transfer permanently onto the plate body.

UNDERGLAZE

Color and/or decoration applied to a bisque-fired plate *before* the transparent glaze is applied for the second firing.

VITRIFICATION

Process by which the clay "body" is subjected to such intense heat that the components melt and fuse to a glassy, non-porous form.

WHITEWARE

Any undecorated white or ivory ceramic. See "Blank."

Index

A

Abstract expressionism, 47-48
Adoration, The, 48
Advertising
  anonymous endorsements in,
    117-18
  clichés in, 118-19
  of collector's plates, 111-24
  an incomplete series, 84-85
  nonsense claims in, 120-21
  pitfalls of, 115-22
  truth in, 112-14, 122-23
  series length, 80-82
Agateware, 10
Age of Steam, The, series, 152
  future value of, 194
American china
  cream-toned, 55
  manufacturers, 13, 56, 58
American Mother's Day series
  future value of, 193, 194
American Panther, 40
American Rose series, 40
Anderson, Robert, 151
Athletes
  in plate art, 204
Austria, 12
  See also Porcelain-producing
    countries

B

Baby's First Step, 27
Backstamps
  artist identification in, 30
  components of, 28-31
  customized, 32-33
  decline of use, 33
  factors concerning, 30-31
  importance of, 27
  maintenance of metal, 178-79
  printing of, 31
  warning on, 31-32
Bannister, Pati
  Lilies of the Field, 42
Baptism of Christ, The, 46
Bareuther, 19
  See also Porcelain houses
Beatles, the, 203
Behind the Frozen Window, 100
Belgium, 12
  See also Porcelain-producing
    countries
Bing & Grøndahl, 12, 202
  backstamp of, 28
  Behind the Frozen Window,
    100
  Christmas in America, 106
  Christmas Remembered, 122
  Dogs and Puppies, 19